Engaging Math Games and Activities for Grades 6-12

Cyndy Davis
Jeanette Gann

Introduction

Engaging Math Games and Activities for Grades 6-12, is a resource to support problem solving as students practice skills in mathematics. Numerous games and activities have been included that span a wide variety of secondary mathematics skills.

Teachers are busy people with numerous responsibilities. Our intention is the creation of ready-to-use games and activities to save teacher time and provide quality materials for mathematics instruction. The materials, directions, and answers for each activity are included for ease of use. **Permission is granted, for those who purchase this book, to print individual pages as needed for their own classroom use.** Teachers will also notice that these game formats could be used to create their own games for another particular skill. In fact, we encourage teachers to adapt these formats for other mathematical concepts under study.

Building skills is an important part of mathematics instruction. It is critical, along with concept building, for mathematical understanding. Mathematical fluency is only achieved by the creation of a balance between conceptual understanding and computational proficiency. These games and activities support the development of computational proficiency and facilitate mathematical thinking.

Many of our students have indicated they had "aha" moments while playing the games, and we have noted in our classrooms a deeper understanding of the mathematical processes through the use of the activities. Enjoy!

Cyndy Davis   **Jeanette Gann**

Engaging Math Games and Activities for Grades 6-12

Table of Contents

Section 1:

Matho

Games

Matho Game Directions

This game is played in a similar manner to Bingo. However, students are grouped so that each student has a partner for this game. Distribute the Matho Game Sheet. Using a <u>pen,</u> both students create a different game card by randomly assigning the numbers 1-30 to the boxes at the top of the sheet. For ease and quickness in checking by the teacher, emphasize to students to write only the number of the answer in the boxes, not the entire answer. Since there are only 25 boxes on the Matho Board, each student will leave out five of the numbers in that range. Each number is to be used only once.

Students will need paper and pencil on which to solve the problems. Each student solves the problem, and then confers with their partner as to the correct answer. Partners help each other to arrive at the correct solution. Teacher puts one problem on the board or overhead at a time, giving partners enough time to solve the problem, find the answer at the bottom of the sheet, and to X out the box on the game board that has the number corresponding to the correct answer. It takes five in a row, diagonally, vertically or horizontally to win.

The answer column on the teacher's page represents the number of the box that should have been crossed off by the student. The teacher checks the student's card using the answer column on the teacher's page to determine if the five numbers in a row were actually ones called by the teacher.

When one student wins, their partner wins as well. Play continues until three winning groups have been determined. The same group may win again if they have a different five in a row combination. Winning groups are rewarded with bonus points or candy at the teacher's discretion.

Solving Proportions

M	A	T	H	O

Directions: Using a pen fill in your card with a random assignment of the numbers from 1-30. You will use only 25 of the 30 numbers. Do not use a number more than once. You will need pencil and paper to work out your answers. Any 5 in a row wins!

1. -15	**7.** $\dfrac{15}{4}$	**13.** 56	**19.** $\dfrac{9}{2}$	**25.** $\dfrac{-16}{5}$
2. 33	**8.** 9450	**14.** 32	**20.** 1750	**26.** 6
3. 3	**9.** 20	**15.** -12	**21.** 42	**27.** 720
4. 270	**10.** $\dfrac{41}{3}$	**16.** -3	**22.** $\dfrac{-7}{10}$	**28.** 10
5. 39600	**11.** $\dfrac{2}{3}$	**17.** $\dfrac{-5}{3}$	**23.** $\dfrac{-15}{4}$	**29.** $\dfrac{-3}{5}$
6. $\dfrac{-1}{10}$	**12.** $\dfrac{3}{5}$	**18.** 25	**24.** -4	**30.** -10

Solving Proportions

	Problem:	Answer:
1.	$\dfrac{x}{4} = \dfrac{3}{2}$	26
2.	$\dfrac{2}{7} = \dfrac{x}{-42}$	15
3.	$\dfrac{-5}{c} = \dfrac{1}{3}$	1
4.	$\dfrac{5}{12} = \dfrac{x+1}{4}$	11
5.	$\dfrac{x}{-3} = \dfrac{3}{-2}$	19
6.	$\dfrac{k}{8} = \dfrac{-2}{5}$	25
7.	$\dfrac{x+2}{7} = \dfrac{5}{7}$	3
8.	$\dfrac{-3}{1} = \dfrac{12}{y}$	24
9.	$\dfrac{4}{5} = \dfrac{3}{w}$	7
10.	$\dfrac{6}{z} = \dfrac{-3}{5}$	30
11.	$\dfrac{x-1}{-4} = \dfrac{2}{3}$	17
12.	$\dfrac{10x}{3} = \dfrac{-2}{6}$	6
13.	$\dfrac{5}{3} = \dfrac{x}{6}$	28
14.	$\dfrac{3}{4} = \dfrac{x}{-5}$	23
15.	Tommy earns $97 in 4 days. How many days will he need to work to earn $485?	9
16.	Sarah saves $52 in 8 weeks. In how many weeks could she have saved $364, if she saved at the same rate?	13

	Problem:	Answer:
17.	A tree casts a shadow of 28 feet, while a 6 foot post nearby casts a shadow of 4 feet. What is the height of the tree?	21
18.	A motorist uses 25 gallons of gasoline in traveling 350 miles. How much gasoline will he use in going 462 miles?	2
19.	A box of crackers lists that 7 crackers are equivalent to 120 calories. How many calories would you consume if you ate the entire box of 42 crackers?	27
20.	Justin sold a total of $630 worth of merchandise in 2 days. If he maintains that average, what will his total sales be for 30 days?	8
21.	You were paid $150 for working 25 hours. How much would you be paid if you worked 45 hours?	4
22.	$\dfrac{350}{x} = \dfrac{5}{25}$	20
23.	$\dfrac{-3}{x} = \dfrac{10}{2}$	29
24.	$\dfrac{4}{5} = \dfrac{x}{40}$	14
25.	$\dfrac{-3}{x+1} = \dfrac{3}{2}$	16
26.	$\dfrac{4}{2x+3} = \dfrac{5}{2}$	22
27.	$\dfrac{5}{x+3} = \dfrac{3}{10}$	10
28.	$\dfrac{7}{5} = \dfrac{35}{x}$	18
29.	$\dfrac{45}{360} = \dfrac{4950}{x}$	5
30.	$\dfrac{2}{5} = \dfrac{x+1}{4}$	12

Solving Linear Equations I

M	A	T	H	O

Directions: Using a pen fill in your card with a random assignment of the numbers from 1-30. You will use only 25 of the 30 numbers. Do not use a number more than once. You will need pencil and paper to work out your answers. Any 5 in a row wins!

1. -5	7. 9	13. 0	19. -9	25. 8
2. 6	8. 4	14. $\dfrac{-1}{2}$	20. -4	26. -24
3. $\dfrac{1}{2}$	9. -40	15. 3	21. -1	27. 15
4. 50	10. 1	16. -3	22. $\dfrac{1}{5}$	28. -8
5. -7	11. -6	17. 10	23. -2	29. 7
6. 11	12. -13	18. 16	24. 5	30. 2

Solving Linear Equations I

Problem:	Answer:	Problem:	Answer:
1. $2x - 11 = 7$	7	16. $6x + 14 = -64$	12
2. $-5x - 8 = 12$	20	17. $11x - 1 = 120$	6
3. $-4x + 5 = -15$	24	18. $-15x = -3$	22
4. $x - 7 = 1$	25	19. $x + 7 = -1$	28
5. $-2x = -6$	15	20. $x - 7 = -1$	2
6. $-10x = 5$	14	21. $-6x + 3 = -9$	30
7. $2x = -18$	19	22. $45 - 13x = 58$	21
8. $4x = 16$	8	23. $-4x + 10 = 38$	5
9. $\dfrac{x}{-20} = 2$	9	24. $1 - 4x = 9$	23
		25. $7 - x = 6$	10
10. $-6x = -3$	3		
11. $2x = -48$	26	26. $\dfrac{x}{-3} = 1$	16
12. $\dfrac{x}{-10} = -5$	4	27. $7x + 15 = -20$	1
13. $x + 15 = 31$	18	28. $\dfrac{x}{-7} + 3 = 2$	29
14. $7 - x = -8$	27	29. $10x - 3 = 97$	17
15. $5 - x = 5$	13	30. $x + 7 = 1$	11

9

M	A	T	H	O

Directions: Using a pen fill in your card with a random assignment of the numbers from 1-30. You will use only 25 of the 30 numbers. Do not use a number more than once. You will need pencil and paper to work out your answers. Any 5 in a row wins!

1. -1	**7.** 16	**13.** -11	**19.** 44	**25.** 6
2. 0	**8.** 20	**14.** 8	**20.** -9	**26.** 7
3. -20	**9.** -36	**15.** $\dfrac{17}{2}$	**21.** 12	**27.** 3
4. -18	**10.** -72	**16.** 14	**22.** -16	**28.** 5
5. 30	**11.** -7	**17.** -8	**23.** -5	**29.** -22
6. $\dfrac{-1}{4}$	**12.** 32	**18.** $\dfrac{16}{3}$	**24.** $\dfrac{3}{8}$	**30.** $\dfrac{5}{2}$

Solving Linear Equations II

1. $-5 = x - (-17)$ **29**

2. $-10 = x - 32 + 6$ **7**

3. $\dfrac{1}{8}x = 4$ **12**

4. $3x = -33$ **13**

5. $6x - 7x = 18$ **4**

6. $4y - 9 = 15$ **25**

7. $13 = 5 - 8m$ **1**

8. $-8 = 32 - 5x$ **14**

9. $\dfrac{1}{3}x + 5 = 9$ **21**

10. $\dfrac{x}{4} + 7 = -2$ **9**

11. $\dfrac{16 - x}{4} = -7$ **19**

12. $10 + v - 17v = 4$ **24**

13. $-n + 5 + 21n = 0$ **6**

14. $6(x - 5) = 12$ **26**

15. $3 + \dfrac{x}{8} = 2$ **17**

16. $3(x + 2) - 4(x - 1) = 10$ **2**

17. $6 + \dfrac{9}{7}x = 24$ **16**

18. $\dfrac{-3}{8}x = -2$ **18**

19. $3(2x + 5) = 30$ **30**

20. $8x = 3x - 35$ **11**

21. $4(5x - 7) = 10x + 2$ **27**

22. $4x + 4 = 2x - 36$ **3**

23. $4x - 2(9 - 3x) = 8x - 1$ **15**

24. $63 - x = 2x + 3$ **8**

25. $6(3x - 5) - 7x = 25$ **28**

26. $2x - 12 - 3x = 60$ **10**

27. $-3(3x + 15) - (10 + x) = 35$ **20**

28. $12 - \dfrac{1}{3}x = 2$ **5**

29. $14x - 8 = 22 + 20x$ **23**

30. $-2(5 + 3m) - 16 = 70$ **22**

Solving Linear Inequalities

M	A	T	H	O

Directions: Using a pen fill in your card with a random assignment of the numbers from 1-30. You will use only 25 of the 30 numbers. Do not use a number more than once. You will need pencil and paper to work out your answers. Any 5 in a row wins!

1. $x \le \dfrac{-5}{9}$	7. $x \le \dfrac{23}{2}$	13. $x < 18$	19. $x \le 1$	25. $x > 1$
2. $x > -6$	8. $x > 2$	14. $x > 4$	20. $x < \dfrac{11}{2}$	26. $x \ge -2$
3. $x \le 5$	9. $x \le -2$	15. $x < -7$	21. $x > -8$	27. $x > -3$
4. $x \ge -1$	10. $x \le 6$	16. $x \le -3$	22. $x \le -4$	28. $x < -10$
5. $x \le 3$	11. $x > 6$	17. $x < -8$	23. $x > 3$	29. $x > -5$
6. $x \le \dfrac{24}{5}$	12. $x < 2$	18. $x < -1$	24. $x > 5$	30. $x \le -6$

Solving Linear Inequalities

Problem:	Answer:
1. $2x - 3 \leq 9$	10
2. $2x - 1 \leq 5$	5
3. $12x + 7 < 2x - 3$	18
4. $2x - 1 < 3$	12
5. $2x + 2 \leq -10$	30
6. $-7 - 2x < 5$	2
7. $1 - x < -5$	11
8. $-3x + 1 \geq 10$	16
9. $5x - 1 > 14$	23
10. $-5x - 3 < 12$	27
11. $-2x - 3x + 2 \leq 7$	4
12. $2x + 4x + 1 + 4 \leq 11$	19
13. $-2x < x - 3$	25
14. $\dfrac{10x + 2}{2} > 11$	8
15. $\dfrac{x}{2} - 1 \leq -2$	9

Problem:	Answer:
16. $\dfrac{7x - 2}{2} \geq -8$	26
17. $2(x + 1) \leq 12$	3
18. $-4(x + 2) > 20$	15
19. $16 + 8x \leq -x - 20$	22
20. $4x + 8 > 3(x + 1)$	29
21. $3x > 2(x + 1) + 3$	24
22. $-7x + 3 \geq 2x + 8$	1
23. $-2x + 2 > -3(x + 2)$	21
24. $3x + 8 + 2x \leq 32$	6
25. $-2x + 7 > 27$	28
26. $8x + 7 > 39$	14
27. $-2x + 4 > 20$	17
28. $3x - x + 4 < 15$	20
29. $x - 7.1 < 10.9$	13
30. $2x + 5 \leq 28$	7

Solving Linear and Absolute Value Equations and Inequalities

M	A	T	H	O

Directions: Using a pen fill in your card with a random assignment of the numbers from 1-30. You will use only 25 of the 30 numbers. Do not use a number more than once. You will need pencil and paper to work out your answers. Any 5 in a row wins!

1. $-2 \leq x \leq 3$	7. $x \geq 7$ or $x \leq -3$	13. $x = 0$ or $x = \dfrac{-8}{3}$	19. $x < 10$	25. $x = 7$ or $x = -3$
2. $6 > x > -2$	8. $x > 3$	14. $x \geq -11\dfrac{1}{2}$	20. $x \geq 3$	26. $x = 12$ or $x = 4$
3. $x \leq 6$	9. $x > \dfrac{2}{3}$ or $x < -2$	15. $x \geq -6$	21. $x \geq 8$ or $x \leq 4$	27. $x \geq 3$ or $x \leq -2$
4. $\varnothing$	10. $x \leq -2$ or $x \geq 6$	16. $x = 12$	22. $-2 < x < 3$	28. $x \geq -1$ or $x \leq -8$
5. $-2 \leq x \leq 12$	11. $\Re$	17. $x > -1$	23. $x \geq 2$ or $x \leq 1$	29. $x \geq 2$
6. $x \geq 6$ or $x \leq 0$	12. $x \geq -4$	18. $x \leq 3$	24. $-8 \leq x \leq -1$	30. $4 \leq x \leq 12$

Solving Linear & Absolute Value Equations & Inequalities

Problem:		Answer:
1.	$2x-1 \le 5$	18
2.	$7-2x \le 19$	15
3.	$-3 < 2x+1 < 7$	22
4.	$\lvert 2x-1 \rvert \le 5$	1
5.	$7(x-3)-1 \ge x-4$	20
6.	$\lvert 2x-4 \rvert \ge 10$	7
7.	$\lvert x-6 \rvert \ge 2$	21
8.	$3(x-6) < 12$	19
9.	$-3\lvert 2x-3 \rvert \le -3$	23
10.	$\lvert 2x+9 \rvert \ge 7$	28
11.	$4x-4 = 3x+8$	16
12.	$\lvert 2x-1 \rvert \ge 5$	27
13.	$\lvert 3x-9 \rvert \ge 9$	6
14.	$\lvert 6-3x \rvert < 12$	2
15.	$\dfrac{8-11x}{4} \le 13$	12
16.	$\lvert x-5 \rvert \le 7$	5

Problem:		Answer:
17.	$\dfrac{\lvert 3x+2 \rvert}{-2} < -2$	9
18.	$\lvert x-8 \rvert = 4$	26
19.	$1-2x < 3$	17
20.	$3(x+14) \ge x-(4+2x)$	14
21.	$3(8-4x) < 9-7x$	8
22.	$\lvert 3x+4 \rvert = 4$	13
23.	$\dfrac{1}{3}(x-3) \le \dfrac{x-2}{4}$	3
24.	$10-2x \le 6$	29
25.	$\lvert x-8 \rvert \le 4$	30
26.	$\lvert 2x-4 \rvert = 10$	25
27.	$\lvert 2x+9 \rvert \le 7$	24
28.	$\lvert 1-3x \rvert = -4$	4
29.	$\lvert 6-3x \rvert \ge 12$	10
30.	$\lvert 3x \rvert > -12$	11

15

Writing Equations of Lines
Write the linear equation that fits the given information:

M	A	T	H	O

Directions: Using a pen fill in your card with a random assignment of the numbers from 1-30. You will use only 25 of the 30 numbers. Do not use a number more than once. You will need pencil and paper to work out your answers. Any 5 in a row wins!

1. $x=1$	**7.** $y=-2$	**13.** $y=4x+9$	**19.** $y=2$	**25.** $y=\dfrac{4}{5}x+4$
2. $y=-4x+3$	**8.** $y=\dfrac{-6}{7}x-\dfrac{18}{7}$	**14.** $y=2x+14$	**20.** $x=3$	**26.** $y=\dfrac{1}{4}x-2$
3. $y=\dfrac{-2}{7}x+10$	**9.** $y=-2x+18$	**15.** $x=5$	**21.** $y=5x-7$	**27.** $y=2x+5$
4. $y=-x$	**10.** $y=5x+18$	**16.** $y=\dfrac{-3}{4}x+\dfrac{1}{4}$	**22.** $y=3$	**28.** $y=\dfrac{1}{5}x-1$
5. $y=\dfrac{2}{3}x-\dfrac{14}{3}$	**11.** $y=\dfrac{5}{2}x+5$	**17.** $y=-2x-11$	**23.** $y=-3x+16$	**29.** $x=-6$
6. $y=\dfrac{3}{4}x+1$	**12.** $y=\dfrac{4}{3}x-\dfrac{1}{2}$	**18.** $y=\dfrac{3}{2}x-3$	**24.** $y=-2x$	**30.** $y=\dfrac{-1}{2}x+6$

Writing Equations of Lines

Problem:	Answer:	Problem:	Answer:
1. m=5; pt. (-2,8)	**10**	**16.** x intercept of 2; b=−3	**18**
2. m=−2; pt. (0,0)	**24**	**17.** vertical line thru (5,1)	**15**
3. pt. (2,-5); pt. (0,3)	**2**	**18.** pt. (6,-2); pt. (3,7)	**23**
4. pt. (-3,-5); pt. (-6,1)	**17**	**19.** m=$\frac{3}{4}$; pt. (4,4)	**6**
5. m=$\frac{-1}{2}$; pt.(8,2)	**30**	**20.** m=5; b=-7	**21**
6. m=-2; pt.(8,2)	**9**	**21.** pt. (-3,0); pt.(4,-6)	**8**
7. m=2; pt.(-3,-1)	**27**	**22.** m=$\frac{2}{3}$; pt. (1,-4)	**5**
8. m=$\frac{-2}{7}$; b=10	**3**	**23.** x intercept of -2; b=5	**11**
9. ‖ to 4x − 3y = 6; pt. (0,-1/2)	**12**	**24.** m=0; pt. (3,2)	**19**
10. m is undefined; pt. (3,2)	**20**	**25.** pt. (-6,1); pt. (-6,3)	**29**
11. x intercept of -5; b=4	**25**	**26.** m is undefined; pt.(1,7)	**1**
12. m=0; pt.(1,-2)	**7**	**27.** pt. (-1,3); pt. (3,3)	**22**
13. x intercept of 8; b=−2	**26**	**28.** m=$\frac{-3}{4}$; pt. (-1,1)	**16**
14. x intercept of 5; b=−1	**28**	**29.** m=4; pt. (-2,1)	**13**
15. pt. (-6,2); pt. (-5,4)	**14**	**30.** m=−1; pt. (0,0)	**4**

Operating with Monomials

M	A	T	H	O

Directions: Using a pen fill in your card with a random assignment of the numbers from 1-30. You will use only 25 of the 30 numbers. Do not use a number more than once. You will need pencil and paper to work out your answers. Any 5 in a row wins!

1. $-6a^2 - 6a$	**7.** $16a^4$	**13.** $\dfrac{-1}{2}a$	**19.** $-4a$	**25.** $9a^2$
2. $\dfrac{3}{a}$	**8.** $8a^2 - 3a$	**14.** $-a^2b^3$	**20.** a	**26.** $-2a - 2b$
3. $\dfrac{-1}{ab^2}$	**9.** $-8a^6b^3$	**15.** $-5a$	**21.** $6a^2b$	**27.** $-2a$
4. $a - b$	**10.** $8ab^2$	**16.** $-8a^2b^2$	**22.** $8a + 2b$	**28.** $-a^2$
5. $-7a - 2b$	**11.** $-8a^3 + 12a^2b$	**17.** $6a^2$	**23.** $2a - 4b$	**29.** $12a^2 - 4ab$
6. $\dfrac{-1}{2a}$	**12.** $4a + 2b$	**18.** $2ab$	**24.** $2a^2b^2$	**30.** $-27a^3b^6$

Operating with Monomials

Problem:	Answer:	Problem:	Answer:
1. $(2a)^4$	7	17. $(-a)(-b)(-ab^2)$	14
2. $(2a)(3a)$	17	18. $\dfrac{-6a^2}{3a}$	27
3. $(3a)^2$	25	19. $\dfrac{-14a^3b}{14ab}$	28
4. $3a(4a) - 2b(2a)$	29		
5. $\dfrac{-4a^4}{8a^5}$	6	20. $\dfrac{-3a^4}{6a^3}$	13
6. $(-a)(-2b)$	18	21. $2a + b + 2a + b$	12
7. $-(3ab^2)^3$	30	22. $\dfrac{-10a^2b^3}{10a^3b^5}$	3
8. $2(a - 2b)$	23	23. $(2a^2)(-4b^2)$	16
9. $-6a(a+1)$	1	24. $(2a)(ab^2)$	24
10. $-4a^2(2a - 3b)$	11	25. $2a + b - a - b$	20
11. $-2(a+b)$	26	26. $\dfrac{-6a^3b^2}{-2a^4b^2}$	2
12. $-2a - 2a$	19		
13. $-7a + 8a - b$	4	27. $-6a - b - a - b$	5
14. $(2a)(2b)(2b)$	10	28. $(-2a)(-3b)(a)$	21
15. $4(2a) + 2(b)$	22	29. $(-2a^2b)^3$	9
16. $4(2a^2) - 3a(1)$	8	30. $-6a - b + a + b$	15

Multiplying & Dividing Monomials with Integer Exponents

M	A	T	H	O

Directions: Using a pen fill in your card with a random assignment of the numbers from 1-30. You will use only 25 of the 30 numbers. Do not use a number more than once. You will need pencil and paper to work out your answers. Any 5 in a row wins!

1. $16a^{10}$	**7.** $\dfrac{12}{a^7}$	**13.** $\dfrac{6}{a^7}$	**19.** $\dfrac{-4}{a^3}$	**25.** $\dfrac{9b^2}{a^4}$
2. a^{10}	**8.** $\dfrac{4}{a^6}$	**14.** $\dfrac{a^6}{16}$	**20.** $\dfrac{16}{a^8}$	**26.** $\dfrac{1}{32a^{10}}$
3. $\dfrac{32}{a^{25}}$	**9.** $\dfrac{-8}{a^2}$	**15.** a^6	**21.** $\dfrac{4a^8}{27b^3}$	**27.** $\dfrac{4a^4}{b^6}$
4. $\dfrac{a^4}{b^8}$	**10.** $-4a^5$	**16.** $\dfrac{16}{a^6}$	**22.** $\dfrac{1}{27a^6b^3}$	**28.** a^3
5. $\dfrac{-a^9}{27}$	**11.** $\dfrac{1}{16a^2b^8}$	**17.** $8a$	**23.** $\dfrac{1}{9a^{10}}$	**29.** $\dfrac{b^6}{16a^4}$
6. $\dfrac{16}{a^{14}}$	**12.** $\dfrac{4}{a^{16}}$	**18.** $\dfrac{8}{a^2}$	**24.** $\dfrac{1}{4a^6}$	**30.** $\dfrac{9}{a^{18}}$

Multiplying & Dividing Monomials with Integer Exponents

Problem:	Answer:	Problem:	Answer:
1. $(2a^3)(-4a^{-5})$	9	17. $(2a^2)(4a^{-1})$	17
2. $\dfrac{-16a^{-6}}{-2a^{-4}}$	18	18. $\dfrac{(a^4)(a^{-1})}{a^{-7}}$	2
3. $(4a^{-3})^{-2}$	14	19. $\dfrac{(6a^{-5})(2a^{-4})}{2a^{-2}}$	13
4. $(2a^3)^{-2}$	24		
5. $(-4a^{-3})^2$	16	20. $\dfrac{-12a^{-4}}{3a^{-1}}$	19
6. $(-4a^5)^2$	1	21. $(-2a^{-3})^2$	8
7. $(\dfrac{3a^{-4}}{a^5})^2$	30	22. $(-4ab^4)^{-2}$	11
		23. $(2a^2)^{-5}$	26
8. $(-2a^{-2})^4$	20		
9. $(-3a^{-3})^{-3}$	5	24. $(\dfrac{a^{-2}}{b^{-4}})^{-2}$	4
10. $(3a^5)^{-2}$	23	25. $(\dfrac{1}{4}a^{-2}b^3)^2$	29
11. $(\dfrac{-4a^{-3}}{a^4})^2$	6	26. $\dfrac{(12a^{-5})(2a^{-4})}{2a^{-2}}$	7
12. $\dfrac{(a^5)(a^{-2})}{a^{-3}}$	15	27. $\left(3a^{-2}b\right)^{-3}(2a)^2$	21
13. $(a^{-3})^{-1}$	28	28. $\dfrac{36a^{-8}}{(-3a^4)^2}$	12
14. $(2a^{-3})(a^5)(-2a^3)$	10		
15. $(3a^2b)^{-3}$	22	29. $(\dfrac{1}{2}a^{-2}b^3)^{-2}$	27
16. $(-3a^{-2}b)^2$	25	30. $(2a^{-3}a^{-2})^5$	3

Multiplying Binomials

M	A	T	H	O

Directions: Using a pen fill in your card with a random assignment of the numbers from 1-30. You will use only 25 of the 30 numbers. Do not use a number more than once. You will need pencil and paper to work out your answers. Any 5 in a row wins!

1. $x^2 + 10x + 21$	**7.** $6x^2 - 11x + 5$	**13.** $6x^2 - x - 5$	**19.** $x^2 - 4$	**25.** $x^2 - 10x + 21$
2. $x^2 - 4x - 21$	**8.** $6x^2 + 11x + 5$	**14.** $8x^2 - 11x + 3$	**20.** $8x^2 - 14x + 3$	**26.** $6x^2 + 11x + 4$
3. $x^2 - 16$	**9.** $6x^2 + 5x - 4$	**15.** $8x^2 + 11x + 3$	**21.** $8x^2 + 5x - 3$	**27.** $x^2 - 4x + 4$
4. $x^2 + 4x + 4$	**10.** $x^2 + 4x - 21$	**16.** $8x^2 - 5x - 3$	**22.** $x^2 + 3x - 4$	**28.** $8x^2 + 14x + 3$
5. $8x^2 + 10x - 3$	**11.** $x^2 + 8x + 16$	**17.** $6x^2 - 5x - 4$	**23.** $x^2 - 3x - 4$	**29.** $x^2 + 5x + 4$
6. $6x^2 + x - 5$	**12.** $8x^2 - 10x - 3$	**18.** $6x^2 - 11x + 4$	**24.** $x^2 - 5x + 4$	**30.** $6x^2 - x - 7$

Multiplying Binomials

Problem:	Answer:	Problem:	Answer:
1. $(2x - 3)(4x - 1)$	**20**	**16.** $(6x - 7)(x + 1)$	**30**
2. $(x + 2)(x - 2)$	**19**	**17.** $(8x + 3)(x + 1)$	**15**
3. $(2x + 3)(4x - 1)$	**5**	**18.** $(x + 4)(x + 1)$	**29**
4. $(x + 3)(x - 7)$	**2**	**19.** $(2x - 1)(3x - 4)$	**18**
5. $(x + 2)^2$	**4**	**20.** $(2x + 1)(3x + 4)$	**26**
6. $(6x + 5)(x + 1)$	**8**	**21.** $(6x - 5)(x + 1)$	**6**
7. $(x - 2)^2$	**27**	**22.** $(x + 4)^2$	**11**
8. $(x + 3)(x + 7)$	**1**	**23.** $(x - 3)(x + 7)$	**10**
9. $(8x - 3)(x - 1)$	**14**	**24.** $(2x - 1)(3x + 4)$	**9**
10. $(x + 4)(x - 4)$	**3**	**25.** $(8x + 3)(x - 1)$	**16**
11. $(8x - 3)(x + 1)$	**21**	**26.** $(x - 4)(x + 1)$	**23**
12. $(6x + 5)(x - 1)$	**13**	**27.** $(2x - 3)(4x + 1)$	**12**
13. $(2x + 1)(3x - 4)$	**17**	**28.** $(x - 3)(x - 7)$	**25**
14. $(6x - 5)(x - 1)$	**7**	**29.** $(2x + 3)(4x + 1)$	**28**
15. $(x - 4)(x - 1)$	**24**	**30.** $(x + 4)(x - 1)$	**22**

Squaring Binomials

M	A	T	H	O

Directions: Using a pen fill in your card with a random assignment of the numbers from 1-30. You will use only 25 of the 30 numbers. Do not use a number more than once. You will need pencil and paper to work out your answers. Any 5 in a row wins!

1. $x^2+10x+25$	**7.** $x^2-10x+25$	**13.** $9x^2+6x+1$	**19.** x^2-4x+4	**25.** $4x^2-8x+4$
2. x^2+6x+9	**8.** $4x^2-4x+1$	**14.** $9x^2+12x+4$	**20.** $x^2-8x+16$	**26.** $16x^2-8x+1$
3. x^2-2x+1	**9.** $4x^2+8x+4$	**15.** $36x^2-24x+4$	**21.** $x^2-12x+36$	**27.** x^4-4x^2+4
4. $x^2-2xy+y^2$	**10.** $4x^2-12x+9$	**16.** x^2+4x+4	**22.** $x^2+2xy+y^2$	**28.** $36x^2-12x+1$
5. x^2+2x+1	**11.** x^4+2x^2+1	**17.** $x^2+8x+16$	**23.** $4x^2+4x+1$	**29.** $9x^2-6x+1$
6. x^2-6x+9	**12.** $25x^2-10x+1$	**18.** $x^2+12x+36$	**24.** $4x^2+12x+9$	**30.** $9x^2-12x+4$

Squaring Binomials

Problem:	Answer:	Problem:	Answer:
1. $(x+1)^2$	5	16. $(x-4)^2$	20
2. $(2x-2)^2$	25	17. $(x+y)^2$	22
3. $(x+2)^2$	16	18. $(x+5)^2$	1
4. $(2x+3)^2$	24	19. $(6x-2)^2$	15
5. $(x+3)^2$	2	20. $(x-2)^2$	19
6. $(x^2+1)^2$	11	21. $(4x-1)^2$	26
7. $(x^2-2)^2$	27	22. $(x-1)^2$	3
8. $(5x-1)^2$	12	23. $(x-y)^2$	4
9. $(3x+1)^2$	13	24. $(x-3)^2$	6
10. $(3x-2)^2$	30	25. $(x+4)^2$	17
11. $(2x-1)^2$	8	26. $(2x+2)^2$	9
12. $(x-5)^2$	7	27. $(x+6)^2$	18
13. $(2x-3)^2$	10	28. $(x-6)^2$	21
14. $(3x-1)^2$	29	29. $(6x-1)^2$	28
15. $(2x+1)^2$	23	30. $(3x+2)^2$	14

Factoring a Difference of Two Squares

M	A	T	H	O

Directions: Using a pen fill in your card with a random assignment of the numbers from 1-30. You will use only 25 of the 30 numbers. Do not use a number more than once. You will need pencil and paper to work out your answers. Any 5 in a row wins!

1. $(6-x)(6+x)$	7. $(1-x)(1+x)$	13. $(x^2-2y)(x^2+2y)$	19. $(2+y)(2-y)$	25. $(2x+5)(2x-5)$
2. $(x-3)(x+3)$	8. $(xy-2)(xy+2)$	14. $(x^2y^4+6)(x^2y^4-6)$	20. $(x+1)(x-1)$	26. $(1-10x)(1+10x)$
3. $(\frac{x}{2}-8)(\frac{x}{2}+8)$	9. $(\frac{x}{2}+\frac{y}{3})(\frac{x}{2}-\frac{y}{3})$	15. $(2x+3y)(2x-3y)$	21. $(x+4)(x-4)$	27. $(x^4+y)(x^4-y)$
4. $(x+5)(x-5)$	10. $(x+2)(x-2)$	16. $(\frac{x^2}{2}+\frac{y^2}{9})(\frac{x^2}{2}-\frac{y^2}{9})$	22. $(7x-8)(7x+8)$	28. $(13+x)(13-x)$
5. $(3x+1)(3x-1)$	11. $(x+y)(x-y)$	17. $(6x^2+7y)(6x^2-7y)$	23. $(x^2+5)(x^2-5)$	29. $(x-10)(x+10)$
6. $(x+\frac{1}{2})(x-\frac{1}{2})$	12. $(xy+1)(xy-1)$	18. $(x^2+10)(x^2-10)$	24. $(x^3+6)(x^3-6)$	30. $(x-12)(x+12)$

Factoring a Difference of Two Squares

Problem:	Answer:	Problem:	Answer:
1. $x^2 - 144$	30	16. $\dfrac{x^2}{4} - \dfrac{y^2}{9}$	9
2. $9x^2 - 1$	5	17. $x^2 - 16$	21
3. $x^4 - 100$	18	18. $4x^2 - 9y^2$	15
4. $x^4 y^8 - 36$	14	19. $169 - x^2$	28
5. $x^2 - \dfrac{1}{4}$	6	20. $\dfrac{x^2}{4} - 64$	3
6. $1 - x^2$	7	21. $x^6 - 36$	24
7. $x^4 - 4y^2$	13	22. $x^2 - 25$	4
8. $36 - x^2$	1	23. $\dfrac{x^4}{4} - \dfrac{y^4}{81}$	16
9. $x^4 - 25$	23	24. $x^2 y^2 - 4$	8
10. $x^2 - 100$	29	25. $x^8 - y^2$	27
11. $36x^4 - 49y^2$	17	26. $x^2 - 4$	10
12. $x^2 - 9$	2	27. $4x^2 - 25$	25
13. $x^2 - y^2$	11	28. $x^2 y^2 - 1$	12
14. $1 - 100x^2$	26	29. $49x^2 - 64$	22
15. $4 - y^2$	19	30. $x^2 - 1$	20

Factoring Quadratic Trinomials with a=1

M	A	T	H	O

Directions: Using a pen fill in your card with a random assignment of the numbers from 1-30. You will use only 25 of the 30 numbers. Do not use a number more than once. You will need pencil and paper to work out your answers. Any 5 in a row wins!

1. $(x+1)(x+1)$	**7.** $(x+6)(x+1)$	**13.** $(x+4)(x+1)$	**19.** $(x+7)(x+3)$	**25.** $(x-3)(x+2)$
2. $(x+4)(x-8)$	**8.** $(x-5)(x-3)$	**14.** $(x+4)(x+4)$	**20.** $(x-4)(x-8)$	**26.** $(x+2)(x+2)$
3. $(x-4)(x+8)$	**9.** $(x-2)(x-2)$	**15.** $(x+4)(x+5)$	**21.** $(x-7)(x-3)$	**27.** $(x-7)(x+3)$
4. $(x-1)(x+6)$	**10.** $(x-4)(x-4)$	**16.** $(x-1)(x-1)$	**22.** $(x-4)(x-5)$	**28.** $(x-3)(x-3)$
5. $(x-1)(x-6)$	**11.** $(x-4)(x+1)$	**17.** $(x+3)(x+3)$	**23.** $(x-4)(x+5)$	**29.** $(x+7)(x-3)$
6. $(x+1)(x-6)$	**12.** $(x-4)(x-1)$	**18.** $(x+4)(x+8)$	**24.** $(x-5)(x+3)$	**30.** $(x+5)(x-3)$

Factoring Quadratic Trinomials with a=1

Problem:	Answer:		Problem:	Answer:
1. $x^2 - x - 6$	25		16. $x^2 + 7x + 6$	7
2. $x^2 + 5x - 6$	4		17. $x^2 - 6x + 9$	28
3. $x^2 - 4x - 21$	27		18. $x^2 - 8x + 15$	8
4. $x^2 - 4x + 4$	9		19. $x^2 + 12x + 32$	18
5. $x^2 + 5x + 4$	13		20. $x^2 - 4x - 32$	2
6. $x^2 + 9x + 20$	15		21. $x^2 - 2x + 1$	16
7. $x^2 - 12x + 32$	20		22. $x^2 + 4x + 4$	26
8. $x^2 + 2x - 15$	30		23. $x^2 - 3x - 4$	11
9. $x^2 + x - 20$	23		24. $x^2 + 6x + 9$	17
10. $x^2 + 2x + 1$	1		25. $x^2 + 10x + 21$	19
11. $x^2 - 5x + 4$	12		26. $x^2 - 9x + 20$	22
12. $x^2 + 8x + 16$	14		27. $x^2 - 8x + 16$	10
13. $x^2 + 4x - 21$	29		28. $x^2 + 4x - 32$	3
14. $x^2 - 2x - 15$	24		29. $x^2 - 5x - 6$	6
15. $x^2 - 7x + 6$	5		30. $x^2 - 10x + 21$	21

Factoring Polynomials Completely

M	A	T	H	O

Directions: Using a pen fill in your card with a random assignment of the numbers from 1-30. You will use only 25 of the 30 numbers. Do not use a number more than once. You will need pencil and paper to work out your answers. Any 5 in a row wins!

1. $(9x^2+4)(3x+2)(3x-2)$	**7.** $(x-y^2)(x^2+xy^2+y^4)$	**13.** $(7x+5)(7x-5)$	**19.** $x(x^2+x+1)$	**25.** $x(x+2)(x-2)$
2. $3(2x+3y)(2x-3y)$	**8.** $y^3(x+2)(x^2-2x+4)$	**14.** $(x-2)(x^2+2x+4)$	**20.** $2x(y-3)(y+2)$	**26.** $10(x+1)(x-1)$
3. $(2x-1)(4x^2+2x+1)$	**9.** $48(x-1)(x^2+x+1)$	**15.** $x(x+9)(x-6)$	**21.** $7(x^2+1)$	**27.** $2x(x+7)(x+3)$
4. $(x^2+9)(x-3)(x+3)$	**10.** $4x^2(x^2+1)(x+1)(x-1)$	**16.** $(5x-2)^2$	**22.** $4(x-4)(x+3)$	**28.** $(2x+1)(x-4)$
5. $(x+5)(x+2)(x-2)$	**11.** $(x^2+2y)(x^4-2x^2y+4y^2)$	**17.** $(2x+1)(x+2y)$	**23.** $(1+10x)(1-10x)$	**29.** $x(x+14)(x-2)$
6. $(4x-3)(16x^2+12x+9)$	**12.** $x^2(x^2+1)(x+1)(x-1)$	**18.** $(5x+6)(x-3)$	**24.** $(x-y)(7+x)$	**30.** $(5+x)(25-5x+x^2)$

Factoring Polynomials Completely

Factor each of the following polynomials completely:

Problem:	Answer:	Problem:	Answer:
1. $4x^6 - 4x^2$	10	16. $25x^2 - 20x + 4$	16
2. $8x^3 - 1$	3	17. $49x^2 - 25$	13
3. $x^4 - 81$	4	18. $2x^3 + 20x^2 + 42x$	27
4. $x^3 + 3x^2 - 54x$	15	19. $125 + x^3$	30
5. $x^6 + 8y^3$	11	20. $x^3y^3 + 8y^3$	8
6. $81x^4 - 16$	1	21. $10x^2 - 10$	26
7. $x^3 + 5x^2 - 4x - 20$	5	22. $x^3 + x^2 + x$	19
8. $2x^2 + 2y + 4xy + x$	17	23. $7x^2 + 7$	21
9. $48x^3 - 48$	9	24. $5x^2 - 9x - 18$	18
10. $12x^2 - 27y^2$	2	25. $7x - 7y + x^2 - xy$	24
11. $2xy^2 - 2xy - 12x$	20	26. $x^3 + 12x^2 - 28x$	29
12. $x^3 - 4x$	25	27. $2x^2 - 7x - 4$	28
13. $x^6 - x^2$	12	28. $1 - 100x^2$	23
14. $64x^3 - 27$	6	29. $x^3 - 8$	14
15. $4x^2 - 4x - 48$	22	30. $x^3 - y^6$	7

Recognizing Geometric Terms

M	A	T	H	O

Directions: Using a pen fill in your card with a random assignment of the numbers from 1-30. You will use only 25 of the 30 numbers. Do not use a number more than once. You will need pencil and paper to work out your answers. Any 5 in a row wins!

1. Perpendicular Lines	7. Same-side Interior Angles	13. Angle Bisector	19. Supplementary Angles	25. Point, Line & Plane
2. Parallel Lines	8. Vertical Angles	14. Complementary Angles	20. Scalene Triangle	26. Perpendicular Bisector
3. 60^0	9. Obtuse Angle	15. Corresponding Angles	21. Equilateral Triangle	27. Quadrilateral
4. Adjacent Angles	10. Congruent Angles	16. Acute Angle	22. Converse	28. Perimeter
5. Skew Lines	11. Right Angle	17. Isosceles Triangle	23. Hypotenuse	29. 180^0
6. Median	12. Diagonal	18. Ray	24. Collinear	30. Midpoint

Recognizing Geometric Terms

Problem:	Answer:
1. Two lines that intersect forming four right angles.	1
2. (Teacher draws two intersecting lines and marks a pair of vertical angles.)	8
3. A triangle having exactly two congruent sides.	17
4. (Teacher draws a pair of parallel lines cut by a transversal and numbers any pair of corresponding angles.)	15
5. (Teacher draws a pair of parallel lines cut by a transversal and numbers any pair of same side interior angles.)	7
6. Two angles whose sum measures $180°$.	19
7. Any four sided figure.	27
8. An angle whose measure is $90°$.	11
9. Angles next to each other that have a common ray and vertex.	4
10. The sum of all three angles in any triangle.	29
11. Two angles whose sum is $90°$.	14
12. The longest side of a right triangle.	23
13. Points on the same line.	24
14. Two lines that are coplanar but do not intersect.	2

Problem:	Answer:
15. Statement that interchanges the hypothesis and conclusion.	22
16. Segment of a triangle from a vertex to the midpoint of the opposite side.	6
17. An angle whose measure is greater than $0°$ but less than $90°$.	16
18. A line that intersects a segment at its midpoint, forming 4 right angles.	26
19. The measure of an angle in an equilateral triangle.	3
20. Distance around a polygon	28
21. Point that divides a line segment into two congruent parts.	30
22. An angle whose measure is greater than $90°$ but less than $180°$.	9
23. Triangle with no equal sides or angles.	20
24. Two lines on different planes that do not intersect.	5
25. Triangle with equal sides and equal angles.	21
26. Line segment through the interior of a polygon, joining opposite vertices.	12
27. Three undefined terms.	25
28. Part of a straight line with one endpoint.	18
29. Two angles having the same measure.	10
30. A ray that divides an angle into two congruent angles.	13

Recognizing Angle Relationships

M	A	T	H	O

Directions: Using a pen fill in your card with a random assignment of the numbers from 1-30. You will use only 25 of the 30 numbers. Do not use a number more than once. You will need pencil and paper to work out your answers. Any 5 in a row wins!

1. 15	7. 32	13. 22	19. 30^0	25. 186
2. 39	8. 60^0	14. 75^0	20. 3	26. 34
3. 44	9. 45^0	15. 180^0	21. 74^0	27. 10
4. 1080^0	10. 13	16. 12	22. 17	28. 144^0
5. 9	11. 50^0	17. 540^0	23. 7	29. 14
6. 360^0	12. 28	18. 90^0	24. 20	30. 11

Recognizing Angle Relationships

Solve for x in the figure when shown.
Figures are not drawn to scale.

Problem:	Answer:
1.	23
2. 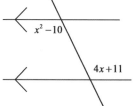	25
3. 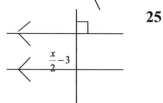	12
4. 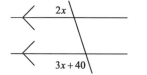	1
5. 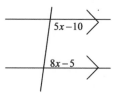	24
6. 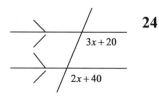	3
7. 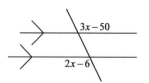	13
8. 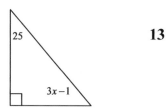	22

Problem:	Answer:
9. 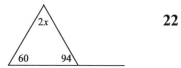	9
10. 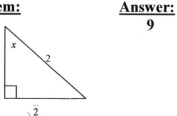	2
11. 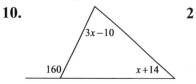	11
12. 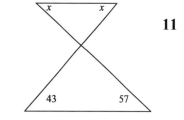	21
13.	14
14. What is the sum of the interior angles of an octagon?	4
15. What is the sum of the interior angles of a pentagon?	17
16. What is the sum of the exterior angles of a heptagon?	6
17. What is the degree measure of each interior angle of a regular decagon?	28

Recognizing Angle Relationships

Problem:	Answer:	Problem:	Answer:

18. What is the degree measure of each exterior angle of a regular hexagon?   **8**

19. What is the number of sides of a dodecagon?   **16**

20. What is the number of vertices of a nonagon?   **5**

21. What is the number of exterior angles of a triangle?   **20**

22. What is the sum of the measures of complementary angles?   **18**

23.    **30**

24. 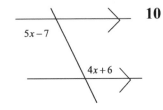   **10**

25. What is the sum of the measures of the angles in a triangle?   **15**

26.   **19**

27. 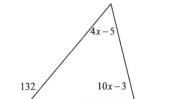   **27**

28. 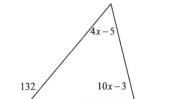   **26**

29.   **29**

30.   **7**

Finding Slope, Distance & Midpoint

M	A	T	H	O

Directions: Using a pen fill in your card with a random assignment of the numbers from 1-30. You will use only 25 of the 30 numbers. Do not use a number more than once. You will need pencil and paper to work out your answers. Any 5 in a row wins!

1. $2\sqrt{34}$	7. $\sqrt{65}$	13. $\dfrac{-1}{3}$	19. $\dfrac{2}{11}$	25. $2\sqrt{29}$
2. $\dfrac{2}{5}$	8. 0	14. $5\sqrt{5}$	20. 6	26. $(7,\dfrac{-3}{2})$
3. undefined	9. $(-7,3)$	15. $\dfrac{1}{8}$	21. 3	27. $(\dfrac{9}{2},\dfrac{1}{2})$
4. $\sqrt{170}$	10. $\sqrt{29}$	16. -6	22. $\dfrac{5}{3}$	28. $(-4,-2)$
5. $2\sqrt{10}$	11. $(-1,-1)$	17. $\sqrt{37}$	23. $(6,4)$	29. $(1,\dfrac{15}{2})$
6. $(\dfrac{-3}{2},6)$	12. 13	18. $\dfrac{-5}{2}$	24. $(\dfrac{5}{2},1)$	30. $(\dfrac{-7}{2},3)$

Finding Slope, Distance & Midpoint

Problem:	Answer:	Problem:	Answer:
1. Find the slope between the points (6,1) and (8,-4).	18	16. Find the slope between the points (6,1) and (6,7).	3
2. Find the midpoint of the points (6,1) and (8,-4).	26	17. Find the midpoint of the points (6,1) and (6,7).	23
3. Find the distance between the points (6,1) and (8,-4).	10	18. Find the distance between the points (6,1) and (6,7).	20
4. Find the slope between the points (-6,-3) and (4,1).	2	19. Find the slope between the points (-7,-1) and (-1,-3).	13
5. Find the midpoint of the points (-6,-3) and (4,1).	11	20. Find the midpoint of the points (-7,-1) and (-1,-3).	28
6. Find the distance between the points (-6,-3) and (4,1).	25	21. Find the distance between the points (-7,-1) and (-1,-3).	5
7. Find the slope between the points (5,7) and (4,-6).	12	22. Find the slope between the points (-2,3) and (-5,3).	8
8. Find the midpoint of the points (5,7) and (4,-6).	27	23. Find the midpoint of the points (-2,3) and (-5,3).	30
9. Find the distance between the points (5,7) and (4,-6).	4	24. Find the distance between the points (-2,3) and (-5,3).	21
10. Find the slope between the points (-10,-2) and (-4,8).	22	25. Find the slope between the points (5,8) and (-3,7).	15
11. Find the midpoint of the points (-10,-2) and (-4,8).	9	26. Find the midpoint of the points (5,8) and (-3,7).	29
12. Find the distance between the points (-10,-2) and (-4,8).	1	27. Find the distance between the points (5,8) and (-3,7).	7
13. Find the slope between the points (-3,0) and (8,2).	19	28. Find the slope between the points (-1,3) and (-2,9).	16
14. Find the midpoint of the points (-3,0) and (8,2).	24	29. Find the midpoint of the points (-1,3) and (-2,9).	6
15. Find the distance between the points (-3,0) and (8,2).	14	30. Find the distance between the points (-1,3) and (-2,9).	17

Finding Values in Special Right Triangles

M	A	T	H	O

Directions: Using a pen fill in your card with a random assignment of the numbers from 1-30. You will use only 25 of the 30 numbers. Do not use a number more than once. You will need pencil and paper to work out your answers. Any 5 in a row wins!

1. 10	**7.** 5	**13.** $4\sqrt{2}$	**19.** 6	**25.** $15\sqrt{2}$
2. $9\sqrt{3}$	**8.** 18	**14.** $6\sqrt{2}$	**20.** $40\sqrt{3}$	**26.** 12
3. 13	**9.** 80	**15.** $20\sqrt{2}$	**21.** $18\sqrt{2}$	**27.** 9
4. 20	**10.** $\dfrac{\sqrt{3}}{2}$	**16.** $\dfrac{10\sqrt{3}}{3}$	**22.** $90\sqrt{2}$	**28.** 16
5. $\dfrac{1}{2}$	**11.** $30\sqrt{3}$	**17.** 15	**23.** $8\sqrt{2}$	**29.** $8\sqrt{3}$
6. $7\sqrt{2}$	**12.** $4\sqrt{3}$	**18.** $20\sqrt{3}$	**24.** $\dfrac{3\sqrt{2}}{2}$	**30.** $3\sqrt{2}$

Finding Values in Special Right Triangles

Find the value of x in each figure. Figures are NOT drawn to scale.

Problem:	Answer:	Problem:	Answer:

1.

30^0 10 x

Answer: **7**

8.

8 30^0 x

Answer: **29**

2.

12 x

Answer: **14**

9.

x 8 30^0

Answer: **28**

3.

x $3\sqrt{2}$

Answer: **19**

10.

$10\sqrt{2}$ x

Answer: **1**

4.

14 x

Answer: **6**

11.

8 x

Answer: **13**

5.

x 6 30^0

Answer: **26**

12.

x 20

Answer: **15**

6.

60^0 x 6

Answer: **12**

13.

3 x 45^0

Answer: **24**

7.

3 45^0 x

Answer: **30**

14.

60^0 18 x

Answer: **2**

40

Finding Values in Special Right Triangles

Problem:	Answer:	Problem:	Answer:	Problem:	Answer:

15.   27

18, 30^0, x

22.   11

30^0, x, 45

29.   10

1, 30^0, x

16.   16

x, 60^0, 5

23.   18

30^0, 40, x

30.   5

1, x, 30^0

17.   8

30^0, x, 9

24.   4

40, 60^0, x

18.   3

30^0, 26, x

25.   20

40, 30^0, x

19.   23

16, x

26.   9

x, 60^0, 40

20.   21

x, 18

27.   25

30, x

21.   22

x, 90

28.   17

x, 7.5, 30^0

41

Evaluating Expressions with Rational Exponents

M	A	T	H	O

Directions: Using a pen fill in your card with a random assignment of the numbers from 1-30. You will use only 25 of the 30 numbers. Do not use a number more than once. You will need pencil and paper to work out your answers. Any 5 in a row wins!

1. $\frac{1}{2}$	7. 15	13. $\frac{5}{7}$	19. 1	25. 81
2. $\frac{-1}{3}$	8. 2	14. $\frac{8}{x}$	20. $\frac{4}{9}$	26. 27
3. $\frac{8}{27}$	9. x^2	15. $\frac{x}{2}$	21. $\frac{9}{4}$	27. $\frac{-1}{6}$
4. $\frac{5}{x^2}$	10. -2	16. $8x$	22. $\frac{-1}{2}$	28. $\frac{1}{6}$
5. 8	11. 64	17. $\frac{3}{5}$	23. $\frac{1}{4}$	29. 6
6. $\frac{1}{8}$	12. -3	18. $\frac{5}{3}$	24. 4	30. $\frac{1}{5}$

42

Evaluating Expressions with Rational Exponents

Problem:	Answer:	Problem:	Answer:
1. $(\frac{9}{25})^{\frac{1}{2}}$	17	16. $(\frac{4}{9})^{\frac{3}{2}}$	3
2. $(\frac{9}{25})^{\frac{-1}{2}}$	18	17. $-(8^{\frac{-1}{6}})^2$	22
3. $(\frac{27}{16})^0$	19	18. $8^{\frac{3}{2}} \bullet 2^{\frac{3}{2}}$	11
4. $(\frac{27}{8})^{\frac{-2}{3}}$	20	19. $(2x^{\frac{-1}{3}})^3$	14
5. $-(4^{\frac{1}{2}})$	10	20. $(\frac{125}{x^6})^{\frac{1}{3}}$	4
6. $4^{\frac{-1}{2}}$	1	21. $\dfrac{x^{\frac{1}{3}}}{2x^{\frac{-2}{3}}}$	15
7. $4^{\frac{3}{2}}$	5	22. $2x^{\frac{3}{2}} \bullet 4x^{\frac{-1}{2}}$	16
8. $(\frac{27}{8})^{\frac{2}{3}}$	21	23. $8^{\frac{2}{3}}$	24
9. $4^{\frac{-3}{2}}$	6	24. $8^{\frac{-2}{3}}$	23
10. $-(9^{\frac{1}{2}})$	12	25. $(9^{\frac{1}{2}})^4$	25
11. $-(9^{\frac{-1}{2}})$	2	26. $125^{\frac{-1}{3}}$	30
12. $15(x^{\frac{3}{4}} \bullet x^{\frac{1}{4}})^0$	7	27. $216^{\frac{1}{3}}$	29
13. $(8^{\frac{-1}{6}})^{-2}$	8	28. $-(216^{\frac{-1}{3}})$	27
14. $(x^{\frac{1}{2}} \bullet x^{\frac{1}{2}})^2$	9	29. $81^{\frac{3}{4}}$	26
15. $(\frac{49}{25})^{\frac{-1}{2}}$	13	30. $216^{\frac{-1}{3}}$	28

Simplifying Radical Expressions

M	A	T	H	O

Directions: Using a pen fill in your card with a random assignment of the numbers from 1-30. You will use only 25 of the 30 numbers. Do not use a number more than once. You will need pencil and paper to work out your answers. Any 5 in a row wins!

1. $2xy\sqrt[5]{3x^4}$	7. $5x^3\sqrt{x}$	13. $5x\sqrt{y}$	19. $\dfrac{3x^2}{2}$	25. $3x^2y^2\sqrt{2y}$
2. $3y\sqrt[3]{x}$	8. $3x$	14. $5x^2y^3\sqrt{2xy}$	20. $\dfrac{x\sqrt[3]{x}}{y}$	26. $2xy\sqrt[3]{3xy^2}$
3. $x\sqrt[4]{8y^3}$	9. $2xy$	15. $4x^3y^5\sqrt{3x}$	21. 9	27. $3y\sqrt[4]{x^3y}$
4. $2xy\sqrt[3]{2x^2y}$	10. $2x^3y$	16. $3x^2\sqrt[3]{3x}$	22. $\dfrac{2}{3}$	28. $2xy^2\sqrt[3]{x}$
5. 8	11. $\dfrac{y\sqrt{5}}{6}$	17. $2xy^2\sqrt{10xy}$	23. $2x^2y\sqrt{2xy}$	29. $\dfrac{3\sqrt{2}}{x}$
6. $2x$	12. $2y\sqrt[3]{2x^2}$	18. $2x^2\sqrt[3]{x^2}$	24. $3x\sqrt[3]{3x}$	30. $8x^3$

44

Simplifying Radical Expressions

Problem:	Answer:	Problem:	Answer:
1. $\sqrt{4x^2y^2}$	9	16. $\sqrt{\dfrac{5y^2}{36}}$	11
2. $\sqrt{48x^7y^{10}}$	15	17. $\sqrt{\dfrac{18}{x^2}}$	29
3. $\sqrt{18x^4y^5}$	25	18. $\sqrt[3]{8^3}$	5
4. $\sqrt[3]{8x^8}$	18	19. $\sqrt[3]{8x^4y^6}$	28
5. $\sqrt[4]{16x^{12}y^4}$	10	20. $\sqrt[3]{16x^2y^3}$	12
6. $\sqrt[3]{16x^5y^4}$	4	21. $\sqrt[4]{81x^3y^5}$	27
7. $\sqrt[3]{24x^4y^5}$	26	22. $\sqrt[4]{8x^4y^3}$	3
8. $\sqrt{\dfrac{9x^4}{4}}$	19	23. $\sqrt[3]{81x^7}$	16
9. $\sqrt[3]{(27)^2}$	21	24. $\sqrt[3]{27x^3}$	8
10. $\sqrt{8x^5y^3}$	23	25. $\sqrt{40x^3y^5}$	17
11. $\sqrt{25x^7}$	7	26. $\sqrt[3]{27xy^3}$	2
12. $\sqrt{50x^5y^7}$	14	27. $\sqrt[3]{81x^4}$	24
13. $\sqrt[3]{\dfrac{x^4}{y^3}}$	20	28. $\sqrt[3]{8x^3}$	6
14. $\sqrt[4]{\dfrac{16}{81}}$	22	29. $\sqrt{25x^2y}$	13
15. $\sqrt[5]{96x^9y^5}$	1	30. $\sqrt{64x^6}$	30

Solving Radical Equations

M	A	T	H	O

Directions: Using a pen fill in your card with a random assignment of the numbers from 1-30. You will use only 25 of the 30 numbers. Do not use a number more than once. You will need pencil and paper to work out your answers. Any 5 in a row wins!

1. $\{4\}$	7. $\{12\}$	13. $\{2\}$	19. $\{57\}$	25. $\{3,7\}$
2. $\{7\}$	8. $\{5\}$	14. $\{23\}$	20. $\{54\}$	26. $\{\frac{1}{16}\}$
3. $\{\pm 3\sqrt{2}\}$	9. $\varnothing$	15. $\{\frac{7}{3}\}$	21. $\{1,-8\}$	27. $\{29\}$
4. $\{9\}$	10. $\{-33\}$	16. $\{39\}$	22. $\{\pm\frac{1}{8}\}$	28. $\{6\}$
5. $\{1\}$	11. $\{162\}$	17. $\{15\}$	23. $\{\pm 2\sqrt{3}\}$	29. $\{13\}$
6. $\{10\}$	12. $\{8\}$	18. $\{11\}$	24. $\{3\}$	30. $\{2,6\}$

Solving Radical Equations

Solve over the $\Re$.

Problem:	Answer:		Problem:	Answer:
1. $\sqrt{2x+3}-7=0$	14		17. $\sqrt{x-4}=5$	27
2. $\sqrt{x^2+3}=x+1$	5		18. $3\sqrt[3]{3x}=2\sqrt[3]{10x+1}$	12
3. $\sqrt{3x}=\sqrt{x+6}$	24		19. $\sqrt{2x+2}=x-3$	2
4. $\sqrt{x+7}-x=1$	13		20. $\sqrt[4]{x^2+4}=2$	23
5. $\sqrt{x-3}+1=\sqrt{2x-5}$	25		21. $\sqrt[4]{\dfrac{1}{x}}=2$	26
6. $\sqrt{x+7}=13$	11		22. $\sqrt{x-3}=6$	16
7. $\sqrt[3]{2x+1}=3$	29		23. $\sqrt[4]{x^2-2}=2$	3
8. $\sqrt{2x-6}=\sqrt{3+x}$	4		24. $\sqrt[3]{\dfrac{1}{x^2}}=4$	22
9. $\sqrt{x+21}-1=\sqrt{x+12}$	1		25. $\sqrt{3x+1}=2\sqrt{x-1}$	8
10. $\sqrt[3]{x+7}=4$	19		26. $\sqrt[3]{x^2+7x}=2$	21
11. $\sqrt[3]{x+6}=-3$	10		27. $\sqrt{5x+6}-\sqrt{3x-2}=2$	30
12. $\sqrt{x-5}=7$	20		28. $3\sqrt{2x+4}=12$	28
13. $\sqrt{2x-4}=4$	6		29. $\sqrt{x^2-36}=\sqrt{9x}$	7
14. $3-\sqrt{x-2}=0$	18		30. $\sqrt[4]{17x+1}=4$	17
15. $7+\sqrt{x-3}=1$	9			
16. $\sqrt[3]{3x+1}=2$	15			

Operating with Algebraic Fractions

M	A	T	H	O

Directions: Using a pen fill in your card with a random assignment of the numbers from 1-30. You will use only 25 of the 30 numbers. Do not use a number more than once. You will need pencil and paper to work out your answers. Any 5 in a row wins!

1.	$\dfrac{21}{x-2}$	7.	$\dfrac{5x-5}{24}$	13.	$\dfrac{x+3}{x-4}$	19.	$\dfrac{2(x+2)}{x^2}$	25.	$\dfrac{5x-4}{3(x+2)(x-2)}$
2.	$\dfrac{8-10z}{5z}$	8.	$\dfrac{1}{4}$	14.	x	20.	1	26.	2
3.	$\dfrac{4x-19}{(x+4)(x-4)}$	9.	$\dfrac{-2}{5z}$	15.	$\dfrac{2}{3(x-2)}$	21.	$\dfrac{5x+2y}{2x^2y}$	27.	$\dfrac{3}{5}$
4.	$\dfrac{5}{2}$	10.	$\dfrac{6x^2y}{z}$	16.	$\dfrac{x+3}{4}$	22.	$\dfrac{3(x+7)}{x-7}$	28.	$\dfrac{5z^2}{3x^2}$
5.	$\dfrac{x-3}{x-4}$	11.	$\dfrac{xy}{4z}$	17.	$\dfrac{24y-2z}{15yz}$	23.	$\dfrac{1}{x-1}$	29.	$\dfrac{2x^2+5x}{(x+2)(x+3)}$
6.	$\dfrac{18x}{(x+9)(x+3)}$	12.	$\dfrac{21}{x-2}$	18.	$\dfrac{x(x+1)}{2(x+5)}$	24.	$\dfrac{x-5}{x-3}$	30.	$\dfrac{x^2-6x+10}{x-3}$

Operating with Algebraic Fractions

Problem:	Answer:	Problem:	Answer:
1. $\dfrac{24x^3y^2}{7z^3} \bullet \dfrac{21z^2}{12xy}$	10	16. $\dfrac{x^2-25}{x^2+11x+30} \bullet \dfrac{x^2+3x-18}{x^2-8x+15}$	20
2. $\dfrac{7}{x^2-4} \bullet \dfrac{2x+4}{21}$	15	17. $\dfrac{8}{5z} - \dfrac{2}{z}$	9
3. $\dfrac{6x^2y^2}{8z} \div 3xy$	11	18. $\dfrac{x^2-7x-8}{2x+2} \bullet \dfrac{5}{x-8}$	4
4. $\dfrac{6x+12}{2x+6} \div \dfrac{x^2-4}{7x+21}$	1	19. $\dfrac{x^2-25}{(x+5)^2} \div \dfrac{2x-10}{4x+20}$	26
5. $\dfrac{6x}{2x^2y} + \dfrac{2x+y}{2x^2y} - \dfrac{3x-y}{2x^2y}$	21	20. $\dfrac{8}{5z} - 2$	2
6. $\dfrac{2}{x-1} - \dfrac{3}{3x-3}$	23	21. $\dfrac{6x+12}{2x+6} \div \dfrac{x^2-4}{7x+21}$	12
7. $\dfrac{3xy}{z^2} \bullet \dfrac{5z^4}{9x^3y}$	28	22. $\dfrac{x^2-49}{x^2y^3} \div \dfrac{x^2-14x+49}{3x^2y^3}$	22
8. $\dfrac{4}{x+4} - \dfrac{3}{x^2-16}$	3	23. $x-3+\dfrac{1}{x-3}$	30
9. $\dfrac{x}{x+2} + \dfrac{x}{x+3}$	29	24. $\dfrac{x}{x-4} - \dfrac{3}{x-4}$	5
10. $\dfrac{x^2-x-2}{(x-2)^2} \div \dfrac{x^3+x^2}{2x^2-8}$	19	25. $\dfrac{x}{x^2-4} + \dfrac{2}{3x+6}$	25
11. $\dfrac{3x-1}{8} - \dfrac{2x+1}{12}$	7	26. $\dfrac{4x+4}{x^2-25} \div \dfrac{8}{x^2-5x}$	18
12. $\dfrac{x^2-5x}{x-1} - \dfrac{4x}{1-x}$	14	27. $\dfrac{2x^2-7x-15}{x^2-8x+15} \bullet \dfrac{3x-15}{6x+9}$	24
13. $\dfrac{x}{x-4} - \dfrac{3}{4-x}$	13	28. $\dfrac{2x^2-6x}{x^2+18x+81} \bullet \dfrac{9x+81}{x^2-9}$	6
14. $\dfrac{8}{5z} - \dfrac{2}{15y}$	17	29. $\dfrac{x^2-2xy-8y^2}{x^2-16y^2} \div \dfrac{5x+10y}{3x+12y}$	27
15. $\dfrac{x-5}{2x-6} - \dfrac{x-7}{4x-12}$	8	30. $\dfrac{x^2+6x+9}{2x^2-18} \div \dfrac{6x+18}{3x^2-27}$	16

Operating with Imaginary Numbers

M	A	T	H	O

Directions: Using a pen fill in your card with a random assignment of the numbers from 1-30. You will use only 25 of the 30 numbers. Do not use a number more than once. You will need pencil and paper to work out your answers. Any 5 in a row wins!

1. 7	7. $26-7i$	13. $\dfrac{-2-16i}{5}$	19. $34+i$	25. 2
2. $-1+4i\sqrt{5}$	8. $-5+i$	14. $5-3i$	20. $-19+6i$	26. $\dfrac{12-i}{15}$
3. $-10i$	9. $-9-6i$	15. $-5-12i$	21. $1-5i$	27. $-7+11i$
4. $12-16i$	10. $\dfrac{2+i}{10}$	16. $8+6i$	22. $\dfrac{9+2i}{17}$	28. $-6+i$
5. $\dfrac{1-i}{2}$	11. $\dfrac{5+3i}{34}$	17. $\dfrac{8+27i}{61}$	23. -3	29. $-8-14i$
6. $2+2i$	12. $-2-10i$	18. i	24. $-32-24i$	30. $2+8i$

Operating with Imaginary Numbers

Simplify fully in a+bi form:

Problem:	Answer:
1. $(-7i-5)-(4-i)$	9
2. i^{65}	18
3. $(3+5i)(1+2i)$	27
4. $3i^{14}$	23
5. $(2+3i)+(-7-2i)$	8
6. $5i-(6+4i)$	28
7. $(4-3i)(5+2i)$	7
8. $\dfrac{3+2i}{6-5i}$	17
9. $(2-6i)^2$	24
10. $\dfrac{1}{4-2i}$	10
11. $(3+i)^2$	16
12. $\dfrac{2+i}{4+i}$	22
13. $(4+i)(1-i)$	14
14. $(4-2i)^2$	4
15. $(3+2i)+(-2-7i)$	21
16. $3i-(2+13i)$	12

Problem:	Answer:
17. $(2-3i)(5+8i)$	19
18. $\dfrac{2-i}{3+i}$	5
19. $(2-3i)^2$	15
20. $\dfrac{4}{1-i}$	6
21. $7i^{20}$	1
22. $2i^{16}$	25
23. $(-3+2i)+(5+6i)$	30
24. $(2i-14)-(5-4i)$	20
25. $\dfrac{5+2i}{6+3i}$	26
26. $(2+i\sqrt{5})^2$	2
27. $-2i(7-4i)$	29
28. $-10i^{101}$	3
29. $\dfrac{1}{5-3i}$	11
30. $\dfrac{6-4i}{1+2i}$	13

Solving Quadratic Equations by Factoring

M	A	T	H	O

Directions: Using a pen fill in your card with a random assignment of the numbers from 1-30. You will use only 25 of the 30 numbers. Do not use a number more than once. You will need pencil and paper to work out your answers. Any 5 in a row wins!

1. $\{2,6\}$	7. $\{\frac{1}{4},\frac{3}{2}\}$	13. $\{0,3\}$	19. $\{-\frac{6}{5},\frac{6}{5}\}$	25. $\{3,-3\}$
2. $\{-\frac{4}{3},3\}$	8. $\{-6,5\}$	14. $\{0,-2\}$	20. $\{\frac{1}{2},-3\}$	26. $\{1,5\}$
3. $\{-1,5\}$	9. $\{4,5\}$	15. $\{-\frac{1}{3},5\}$	21. $\{-\frac{7}{3},-2\}$	27. $\{9,-9\}$
4. $\{0,6\}$	10. $\{-5,2\}$	16. $\{4\}$	22. $\{0,7\}$	28. $\{-\frac{1}{2},2\}$
5. $\{-2,7\}$	11. $\{3,-4\}$	17. $\{-2,-4\}$	23. $\{-\frac{1}{6},1\}$	29. $\{0,5\}$
6. $\{-5,5\}$	12. $\{-3,5\}$	18. $\{6\}$	24. $\{2,5\}$	30. $\{-2,-\frac{3}{4}\}$

Solving Quadratic Equations by Factoring

Problem:	Answer:	Problem:	Answer:
1. $x^2 + 6x + 8 = 0$	17	16. $x^2 - 7x = -10$	24
2. $x^2 - 9x + 20 = 0$	9	17. $x^2 - 25 = 0$	6
3. $x^2 - 5x = 0$	29	18. $x^2 - 5x = 14$	5
4. $4x^2 - 36 = 0$	25	19. $x^2 - 6x + 5 = 0$	26
5. $x^2 = 8x - 12$	1	20. $x^2 - 2x - 15 = 0$	12
6. $8x^2 - 14x + 3 = 0$	7	21. $3x^2 + 13x = -14$	21
7. $x^2 - 7x = 0$	22	22. $x^2 = 6x$	4
8. $6x^2 + 12x = 0$	14	23. $x^2 = 81$	27
9. $x^2 - 12x + 36 = 0$	18	24. $3x^2 - 14x - 5 = 0$	15
10. $x^2 + x = 30$	8	25. $6x^2 - 5x - 1 = 0$	23
11. $x^2 - 8x + 16 = 0$	16	26. $4x^2 + 11x + 6 = 0$	30
12. $2x^2 + 6x - 20 = 0$	10	27. $x^2 + x - 12 = 0$	11
13. $3x^2 - 5x - 12 = 0$	2	28. $2x^2 + 5x - 3 = 0$	20
14. $25x^2 - 36 = 0$	19	29. $2x^2 - 3x - 2 = 0$	28
15. $x(x - 3) = 0$	13	30. $x^2 - 4x = 5$	3

Solving Quadratic Equations by the Quadratic Formula

M	A	T	H	O

Directions: Using a pen fill in your card with a random assignment of the numbers from 1-30. You will use only 25 of the 30 numbers. Do not use a number more than once. You will need pencil and paper to work out your answers. Any 5 in a row wins!

1.	$\{-3\pm\sqrt{3}\}$	**7.**	$\{\dfrac{1\pm\sqrt{17}}{4}\}$	**13.**	$\{\dfrac{1\pm i\sqrt{3}}{2}\}$	**19.**	$\{\dfrac{3\pm i\sqrt{3}}{6}\}$	**25.**	$\{1\pm\sqrt{5}\}$
2.	$\{\dfrac{1\pm 5i}{2}\}$	**8.**	$\{-4\pm 3i\}$	**14.**	$\{\dfrac{-1\pm i\sqrt{5}}{2}\}$	**20.**	$\{2\pm\sqrt{6}\}$	**26.**	$\{\dfrac{2\pm 3\sqrt{2}}{2}\}$
3.	$\{5\pm 3\sqrt{5}\}$	**9.**	$\{\dfrac{3\pm\sqrt{3}}{3}\}$	**15.**	$\{4\pm\sqrt{5}\}$	**21.**	$\{\dfrac{-5\pm\sqrt{73}}{6}\}$	**27.**	$\{-1\pm\sqrt{2}\}$
4.	$\{\dfrac{-2\pm\sqrt{3}}{2}\}$	**10.**	$\{\dfrac{5}{3},\dfrac{3}{2}\}$	**16.**	$\{\dfrac{3\pm\sqrt{33}}{4}\}$	**22.**	$\{\dfrac{1\pm 2\sqrt{2}}{3}\}$	**28.**	$\{\dfrac{-7}{2},3\}$
5.	$\{\dfrac{-3\pm\sqrt{33}}{4}\}$	**11.**	$\{1\pm i\sqrt{2}\}$	**17.**	$\{\dfrac{-5\pm\sqrt{73}}{6}\}$	**23.**	$\{\dfrac{3\pm\sqrt{37}}{2}\}$	**29.**	$\{2\pm\sqrt{2}\}$
6.	$\{4\pm 2\sqrt{5}\}$	**12.**	$\{\dfrac{2\pm i\sqrt{2}}{3}\}$	**18.**	$\{\pm 4i\}$	**24.**	$\{\dfrac{3\pm i\sqrt{3}}{2}\}$	**30.**	$\{\dfrac{5\pm\sqrt{13}}{2}\}$

Solving Quadratic Equations by the Quadratic Formula

Problem:	Answer:	Problem:	Answer:
1. $x^2 - 8x = 4$	6	16. $x^2 + 16 = 0$	18
2. $x^2 - 4x - 2 = 0$	20	17. $x^2 - x + 1 = 0$	13
3. $x^2 - 5x + 3 = 0$	30	18. $2x^2 - 4x - 7 = 0$	26
4. $2x^2 = x + 2$	7	19. $x^2 + 8x = -25$	8
5. $2x^2 - 3x - 3 = 0$	16	20. $6x^2 - 19x + 15 = 0$	10
6. $x^2 - 2x - 4 = 0$	25	21. $x^2 - 8x + 11 = 0$	15
7. $x^2 + 2x - 1 = 0$	27	22. $x^2 - 3x - 7 = 0$	23
8. $x^2 = -6x - 6$	1	23. $2x^2 + x = 21$	28
9. $x^2 - 2x + 3 = 0$	11	24. $9x^2 = 6x + 7$	22
10. $3x^2 = -5x + 4$	17	25. $4x^2 + 8x = -1$	4
11. $3x^2 + 2 = 4x$	12	26. $3x^2 = -5x + 4$	21
12. $3x^2 - 3x + 1 = 0$	19	27. $3x^2 - 6x + 2 = 0$	9
13. $2x^2 - 2x + 13 = 0$	2	28. $2x^2 + 2x = -3$	14
14. $x^2 - 3x + 3 = 0$	24	29. $x^2 - 10x - 20 = 0$	3
15. $x^2 + 2 = 4x$	29	30. $2x^2 + 3x = 3$	5

Finding Amplitude, Period & Translations for Graphing Trig Functions

M	A	T	H	O

Directions: Using a pen fill in your card with a random assignment of the numbers from 1-30. You will use only 25 of the 30 numbers. Do not use a number more than once. You will need pencil and paper to work out your answers. Any 5 in a row wins!

1. $a = 1; p = \dfrac{\pi}{2};$ $ht = 0; vt = 0$	**7.** $a = 2; p = \pi;$ $ht = 0; vt = 0$	**13.** $a = 1; p = 2\pi;$ $ht = 0; vt = 0$	**19.** $a = 4; p = 2\pi;$ $ht = -180^0; vt = 0$	**25.** $a = 6; p = \dfrac{2\pi}{3};$ $ht = 0; vt = 1$
2. $a = 2; p = \dfrac{\pi}{3};$ $ht = -50^0; vt = 0$	**8.** $a = 4; p = \dfrac{\pi}{2};$ $ht = 0; vt = 0$	**14.** $a = 3; p = 2\pi;$ $ht = \dfrac{-\pi}{2}; vt = 0$	**20.** $a = 2; p = 6\pi;$ $ht = -300^0; vt = 0$	**26.** $a = 6; p = 2\pi;$ $ht = 0; vt = 0$
3. $a = 2; p = 2\pi;$ $ht = 90^0; vt = 0$	**9.** $a = 4; p = \pi;$ $ht = -45^0; vt = 0$	**15.** $a = 1; p = 2\pi;$ $ht = -90^0; vt = 0$	**21.** $a = 2; p = 4\pi;$ $ht = 60^0; vt = 0$	**27.** $a = 2; p = 2\pi;$ $ht = 0; vt = 0$
4. $a = 6; p = \dfrac{2\pi}{3};$ $ht = 0; vt = 0$	**10.** $a = 3; p = \pi;$ $ht = 0; vt = 0$	**16.** $a = 4; p = \dfrac{2\pi}{3};$ $ht = 0; vt = 1$	**22.** $a = 3; p = \dfrac{\pi}{2};$ $ht = 0; vt = 0$	**28.** $a = 2; p = \dfrac{\pi}{2};$ $ht = \dfrac{\pi}{4}; vt = 0$
5. $a = 6; p = \pi;$ $ht = 90^0; vt = 0$	**11.** $a = 1; p = \dfrac{2\pi}{3};$ $ht = 0; vt = 0$	**17.** $a = 4; p = \pi;$ $ht = 0; vt = 0$	**23.** $a = 3; p = 4\pi;$ $ht = 0; vt = 0$	**29.** $a = 2; p = 2\pi;$ $ht = 0; vt = 1$
6. $a = 3; p = 2\pi;$ $ht = 0; vt = 0$	**12.** $a = 6; p = \pi;$ $ht = 0; vt = 0$	**18.** $a = 3; p = \pi;$ $ht = 90^0; vt = 0$	**24.** $a = 3; p = 2\pi;$ $ht = 0; vt = 1$	**30.** $a = 3; p = 2\pi;$ $ht = 180^0; vt = 0$

Finding Amplitude, Period & Translations for Graphing Trig Functions

For the given trigonometric function name the amplitude, period, horizontal translation and vertical translation:

Problem:	Answer:	Problem:	Answer:
1. $y = 3\sin\theta$	6	16. $y = 3\cos\theta + 1$	24
2. $y = 3\cos 2\theta$	10	17. $y = 3\cos 4\theta$	22
3. $y = -3\sin(\theta + \frac{\pi}{2})$	14	18. $y = 6\sin 2\theta$	12
		19. $y = -6\cos 3\theta$	4
4. $y = 2\sin(\frac{1}{3}\theta + 100^0)$	20	20. $y = 2\cos 2\theta$	7
5. $y = -2\cos\theta + 1$	29	21. $y = 6\sin 3\theta + 1$	25
6. $y = \cos 3\theta$	11	22. $y = -6\cos\theta$	26
7. $y = -2\cos(\frac{1}{2}\theta - 30^0)$	21	23. $y = \cos\theta$	13
		24. $y = 2\sin\theta$	27
8. $y = 3\sin(2\theta - 180^0)$	18	25. $y = -6\cos(2\theta - 180^0)$	5
9. $y = -\sin 4\theta$	1	26. $y = 4\sin 2\theta$	17
10. $y = 3\sin\frac{1}{2}\theta$	23	27. $y = -4\cos(\theta + 180^0)$	19
11. $y = 2\cos(\theta - 90^0)$	3	28. $y = 4\cos 3\theta + 1$	16
12. $y = -\cos(\theta + 90^0)$	15	29. $y = -4\cos 4\theta$	8
13. $y = 2\sin(4\theta - \pi)$	28	30. $y = -4\sin(2\theta + 90^0)$	9
14. $y = -2\cos(6\theta + 300^0)$	2		
15. $y = 3\sin(180^0 - \theta)$	30		

Evaluating Inverse Trigonometric Functions

M	A	T	H	O

Directions: Using a pen fill in your card with a random assignment of the numbers from 1-30. You will use only 25 of the 30 numbers. Do not use a number more than once. You will need pencil and paper to work out your answers. Any 5 in a row wins!

1. $2\sqrt{2}$	**7.** 1	**13.** $\dfrac{5\pi}{6}$	**19.** $\dfrac{\sqrt{3}}{2}$	**25.** $\dfrac{-\pi}{6}$
2. $\dfrac{12}{13}$	**8.** $\dfrac{\pi}{2}$	**14.** $\dfrac{\sqrt{2}}{2}$	**20.** -1	**26.** $\varnothing$
3. 5	**9.** 0	**15.** $\dfrac{1}{2}$	**21.** $\dfrac{-2}{\sqrt{29}}$	**27.** $\dfrac{2\sqrt{2}}{3}$
4. $\dfrac{-2}{3}$	**10.** $\dfrac{\sqrt{13}}{3}$	**16.** $\dfrac{4}{5}$	**22.** $\dfrac{-\sqrt{2}}{2}$	**28.** $\dfrac{3\pi}{4}$
5. $\dfrac{\sqrt{5}}{3}$	**11.** $\dfrac{15}{17}$	**17.** $\dfrac{\pi}{3}$	**23.** $\dfrac{2\pi}{3}$	**29.** $\dfrac{-\pi}{2}$
6. π	**12.** $\dfrac{-\pi}{3}$	**18.** $\dfrac{-\pi}{4}$	**24.** $\dfrac{\pi}{6}$	**30.** $\dfrac{1}{3}$

Evaluating Inverse Trigonometric Functions

Evaluate under the principal values of the function:

Problem:	Answer:	Problem:	Answer:
1. $\sin^{-1}(\frac{-1}{2})$	25	16. $\cos(\arcsin\frac{1}{2})$	19
2. $\arccos(-1)$	6	17. $\sin(\arccos\frac{-2}{3})$	5
3. $\tan^{-1}(-1)$	18	18. $\cos^{-1}(\sin\frac{-\pi}{6})$	23
4. $\sin^{-1}(\sin\frac{3\pi}{2})$	29	19. $\sec(\arctan\frac{2}{3})$	10
5. $\cos(\arccos\frac{-2}{3})$	4	20. $\sin(\arctan-1)$	22
6. $\sin^{-1}(\sin\frac{\pi}{3})$	17	21. $\sin(\arccos\frac{5}{13})$	2
7. $\arcsin 5$	26	22. $\cos(\tan^{-1}\frac{-3}{4})$	16
8. $\tan(\tan^{-1}5)$	3	23. $\sin(\arccos\frac{\sqrt{3}}{2})$	15
9. $\sin(\tan^{-1}\frac{-2}{5})$	21	24. $\cos(\sin^{-1}\frac{8}{17})$	11
10. $\arcsin\frac{-\sqrt{3}}{2}$	12	25. $\cos(\cos^{-1}\frac{1}{3})$	30
11. $\cos^{-1}\frac{-\sqrt{3}}{2}$	13	26. $\sin(\sin^{-1}1)$	7
12. $\arccos(\sin\frac{2\pi}{3})$	24	27. $\sin(\arccos\frac{1}{3})$	27
13. $\operatorname{arc cot}(-1)$	28	28. $\tan(arc\tan-1)$	20
14. $\arccos 1$	9	29. $\arcsin 1$	8
15. $\sin(\cos^{-1}\frac{-\sqrt{2}}{2})$	14	30. $\tan(\arccos\frac{1}{3})$	1

Evaluating Logarithmic Expressions & Equations

M	A	T	H	O

Directions: Using a pen fill in your card with a random assignment of the numbers from 1-30. You will use only 25 of the 30 numbers. Do not use a number more than once. You will need pencil and paper to work out your answers. Any 5 in a row wins!

1. 2	**7.** 36	**13.** 10	**19.** 7	**25.** -5
2. 4	**8.** 100	**14.** -3	**20.** 8	**26.** 12
3. 3	**9.** e^2	**15.** 16	**21.** -2	**27.** 1,000
4. -1	**10.** 11	**16.** e^{20}	**22.** 27	**28.** 64
5. $\frac{1}{2}$	**11.** 5	**17.** -4	**23.** 1	**29.** 9
6. 25	**12.** 6	**18.** $\frac{1}{3}$	**24.** $\frac{1}{36}$	**30.** 0

Evaluating Logarithmic Expressions & Equations

Problem:	Answer:
1. $\log_2 32$	11
2. $\log_2 64$	12
3. $\log_2 2^{10}$	13
4. $\log_7 49$	1
5. Solve: $\log_x 121 = 2$	10
6. Solve: $\log_x 64 = 2$	20
7. $\log_2 \frac{1}{4}$	21
8. $\log_5 \sqrt[3]{5}$	18
9. $\log_2 16$	2
10. Solve: $\log_6 x = 2$	7
11. Solve: $\log x = 2$	8
12. Solve: $\ln x = 20$	16
13. $\log_2 2^9$	29
14. $\log_5 \sqrt{5}$	5
15. Solve: $\log_4 x = 2$	15

Problem:	Answer:
16. Solve: $\log x = 3$	27
17. $\log .0001$	17
18. Solve: $\log_6 x = -2$	24
19. $\log_2 \frac{1}{8}$	14
20. Solve: $\ln x = 2$	9
21. $\ln e^{12}$	26
22. $\log_4 64$	3
23. $\log_5 1$	30
24. $\log 10^7$	19
25. Solve: $\log_9 x = \frac{3}{2}$	22
26. $\log_5 \frac{1}{5}$	4
27. Solve: $\log_5 x = 2$	6
28. Solve: $\ln x = 0$	23
29. Solve: $\log_4 x = 3$	28
30. $\log_2 \frac{1}{32}$	25

61

Finding Derivatives using the Power Rule

M	A	T	H	O

Directions: Using a pen fill in your card with a random assignment of the numbers from 1-30. You will use only 25 of the 30 numbers. Do not use a number more than once. You will need pencil and paper to work out your answers. Any 5 in a row wins!

1. $6x-2$	7. $x+1$	13. $-9x^{-4}+40x^{-9}$	19. $3\sqrt{2}x^2-x$	25. $\dfrac{-1}{3}$
2. $9x^2-12x+10$	8. $\dfrac{1}{4}-20x^{-6}+21x^{-8}$	14. $-2x-2+2x^{-3}$	20. $3x^2-16x+7$	26. $6x^2+6x-4-4x^{-3}$
3. $9x^8+6x^2-4x$	9. $\dfrac{-2}{x^2}-\dfrac{12}{x^4}-6$	15. $3x^2-4+\dfrac{6}{x^4}$	21. -3	27. $8x^{\frac{-1}{2}}$
4. $6x+2$	10. $7x^6+8x^3-3$	16. $-30x^{-11}-2$	22. $-4-6x^2$	28. $\dfrac{1}{\sqrt{x}}+7$
5. $7x^6+8x^3-9x^2$	11. $\dfrac{4}{x^3}-\dfrac{12}{x^4}$	17. $8x^3-6x-\dfrac{10}{7x^3}$	23. $-2+14x$	29. $x^{\frac{5}{4}}+1x^{-3}+x^{\frac{-3}{4}}$
6. $9x^2+6$	12. $5x^4+12$	18. $3\sqrt{6}x^2-4x$	24. $80x^4-12x^3+12x$	30. $3x^2+8x-2$

Finding Derivatives using the Power Rule

Find the first derivative of each of the following:

Problem:	Answer:	Problem:	Answer:
1. $\dfrac{x}{4}+\dfrac{4}{x^5}-\dfrac{3}{x^7}$	8	16. $x^3-4x-\dfrac{2}{x^3}$	15
2. $2x^4-3x^2+\dfrac{5}{7x^2}$	17	17. $16\sqrt{x}+7$	27
3. $x^7+2x^4-3x^3$	5	18. $\dfrac{4}{9}x^{\frac{9}{4}}-\dfrac{1}{2}x^{-2}+4x^{\frac{1}{4}}$	29
4. $\dfrac{x^2}{2}+x$	7	19. x^3+4x^2-2x	30
5. $16x^5-3x^4+6x^2-4$	24	20. $3x^2-2x+1$	1
6. x^7+2x^4-3x+5	10	21. $2\sqrt{x}+7x$	28
7. $3x^3+6x+\pi$	6	22. $1-2x+7x^2$	23
8. $\dfrac{-2}{x^2}+\dfrac{4}{x^3}$	11	23. x^3-8x^2+7x-6	20
9. $\sqrt{10}-3x$	21	24. $\sqrt{6}x^3-2x^2+5$	18
10. $3x^3-6x^2+10x-5$	2	25. $\dfrac{3}{x^{10}}-2x$	16
11. $2x^3+3x^2-4x+\dfrac{2}{x^2}$	26	26. $x^5+12x-4$	12
12. $7-4x-2x^3$	22	27. $\sqrt{2}x^3-\dfrac{1}{2}x^2$	19
13. $\dfrac{2}{x}+\dfrac{4}{x^3}-6x-7$	9	28. $-x^2-2x-\dfrac{1}{x^2}$	14
14. $x^9+2x^3-2x^2$	3	29. $3x^{-3}-5x^{-8}$	13
15. $1-\dfrac{x}{3}$	25	30. $3x^2+2x+2$	4

63

Finding Derivatives using the Composite Rule

M	A	T	H	O

Directions: Using a pen fill in your card with a random assignment of the numbers from 1-30. You will use only 25 of the 30 numbers. Do not use a number more than once. You will need pencil and paper to work out your answers. Any 5 in a row wins!

1. $\dfrac{-2\cos 2x}{\sin^2 2x}$	**7.** $2\sin x \cos x$	**13.** $(50x-10)(5x^2-2x+3)^4$	**19.** $4\sin x \cos x$	**25.** $2\cos 2x$
2. $6\sin 3x$	**8.** $\dfrac{-16}{(2x+5)^3}$	**14.** $(-2x-2)(x^2+2x+9)^{-2}$	**20.** $2(x+\sin x)(1+\cos x)$	**26.** $10\sin^4 x \cos x$
3. $-18(3x+2)^2$	**9.** $-4(2x-3)^{-3}$	**15.** $\dfrac{33(2x-1)^2}{(5x+3)^4}$	**21.** $-12\sin x \cos^2 x$	**27.** $\dfrac{5}{(3x+1)^2}$
4. $\dfrac{-10}{(x-3)^3}$	**10.** $\dfrac{-30x^4}{(2x^5-7)^4}$	**16.** $(24x+7)(3x-1)^2$	**22.** $-6\cos 3x$	**28.** $\dfrac{20}{(5x-3)^5}$
5. $\dfrac{-15\sin x}{\cos^4 x}$	**11.** $12\sin x \cos x$	**17.** $(8x-1)(2x+5)^2$	**23.** $-18\sin^2 x \cos x$	**29.** $\dfrac{-4\cos x}{\sin^3 x}$
6. $-9(4-3x)^2$	**12.** $24x-60$	**18.** $\dfrac{8\sin x}{\cos^3 x}$	**24.** $4(2x+1)^3$	**30.** $-15(4-3x)^4$

64

Finding Derivatives using the Composite Rule

Find the first derivative of each of the following:

Problem:		Answer:		Problem:		Answer:

1. $y = 3(2x-5)^2$ — 12

2. $y = -2(3x+2)^3$ — 3

3. $y = \dfrac{1}{2}(2x+1)^4$ — 24

4. $y = 6(\sin x)^2$ — 11

5. $y = -2\cos^2 x$ — 19

6. $y = -6\sin^3 x$ — 23

7. $y = \dfrac{1}{(2x^5-7)^3}$ — 10

8. $y = \dfrac{5}{(x-3)^2}$ — 4

9. $y = (5x^2-2x+3)^5$ — 13

10. $y = \left(\dfrac{2x-1}{5x+3}\right)^3$ — 15

11. $y = \sin 2x$ — 25

12. $y = -2\cos 3x$ — 2

13. $y = -2\sin 3x$ — 22

14. $y = (x+\sin x)^2$ — 20

15. $y = \dfrac{1}{\sin 2x}$ — 1

16. $y = (4-3x)^5$ — 30

17. $y = \dfrac{1}{(2x-3)^2}$ — 9

18. $y = \dfrac{1}{x^2+2x+9}$ — 14

19. $y = (2x+1)(3x-1)^3$ — 16

20. $y = \sin^2 x$ — 7

21. $y = (x-1)(2x+5)^3$ — 17

22. $y = \dfrac{2x-1}{3x+1}$ — 27

23. $y = \dfrac{2}{\sin^2 x}$ — 29

24. $y = \dfrac{-5}{\cos^3 x}$ — 5

25. $y = \dfrac{4}{\cos^2 x}$ — 18

26. $y = \dfrac{4}{(2x+5)^2}$ — 8

27. $y = \dfrac{-1}{(5x-3)^4}$ — 28

28. $y = (4-3x)^3$ — 6

29. $y = 2\sin^5 x$ — 26

30. $y = 4\cos^3 x$ — 21

Finding Derivatives of Calculus Functions

M	A	T	H	O

Directions: Using a pen fill in your card with a random assignment of the numbers from 1-30. You will use only 25 of the 30 numbers. Do not use a number more than once. You will need pencil and paper to work out your answers. Any 5 in a row wins!

1. $\dfrac{-1}{2x^2}+2$	7. $-12x^2+6$	13. $\dfrac{9}{x^4}$	19. $\dfrac{-2}{(2x+1)^2}$	25. $\dfrac{2}{(x+1)^2}$
2. $12x^8$	8. $\dfrac{-1}{(x-3)^2}$	14. $\dfrac{-8x+3}{(4x^2-3x+9)^2}$	20. $\dfrac{-2}{(x-1)^2}$	26. $6x^5+4x^3-2x$
3. $5x^4+6x^2+2x$	9. $\dfrac{-3}{(x-3)^2}$	15. $\dfrac{-15}{x^6}-\dfrac{6}{x^4}$	21. 6	27. $\dfrac{-18x}{(3x^2+1)^2}$
4. $12x^3-3$	10. $2\pi x$	16. $\dfrac{-5x^2-1}{(5x^2-1)^2}$	22. $\dfrac{-20x}{(5x^2-1)^2}$	28. 0
5. $\dfrac{-6x}{(3x^2+1)^2}$	11. $3x^2+1$	17. $\dfrac{1}{(x+1)^2}$	23. $\dfrac{1}{(2x+1)^2}$	29. $5x^4+42x^2+2x-51$
6. $-6\sqrt{x}-\sqrt{2}$	12. $8x+4$	18. $\dfrac{-3}{x^6}$	24. $40x^3-12x^2$	30. $\dfrac{-1}{(x-1)^2}$

Finding Derivatives of Calculus Functions

Find the first derivative of each of the following functions:

Problem:		Answer:	Problem:		Answer:
1.	$y = -4x^3 + 6x - 6$	7	16.	$f(x) = \frac{4}{3}x^9$	2
2.	$y = x(x^2 + 1)$	11	17.	$f(x) = (2x+1)^2$	12
3.	$y = 3x(x^3 - 1)$	4	18.	$f(x) = \frac{x}{x+1}$	17
4.	$f(x) = (x^2 + 2)(x^3 + 1)$	3			
5.	$f(x) = 6x + 1$	21	19.	$y = \pi x^2$	10
6.	$f(x) = -4\sqrt{x^3} - \sqrt{2}x$	6	20.	$y = 10x^4 - 4x^3$	24
7.	$y = \frac{1}{3x^2 + 1}$	5	21.	$y = \frac{x}{5x^2 - 1}$	16
8.	$y = \frac{3}{x^5} + \frac{2}{x^3}$	15	22.	$y = \frac{-3}{x^3}$	13
9.	$y = \frac{2x - 1}{x - 1}$	30	23.	$y = \frac{1}{4x^2 - 3x + 9}$	14
10.	$y = \frac{3}{5x^5}$	18	24.	$y = \frac{1}{x - 3}$	8
11.	$y = \frac{2}{5x^2 - 1}$	22	25.	$y = \frac{x}{x - 3}$	9
12.	$y = \frac{3}{3x^2 + 1}$	27	26.	$y = \frac{1}{2x} + 2x$	1
13.	$y = \frac{x - 1}{x + 1}$	25	27.	$f(x) = (x^4 - 1)(x^2 + 1)$	26
			28.	$y = (x^2 + 17)(x^3 - 3x + 1)$	29
14.	$y = \frac{x}{2x + 1}$	23	29.	$y = \frac{1}{2x + 1}$	19
15.	$y = \frac{x + 1}{x - 1}$	20	30.	$y = \pi^3$	28

67

Integrating Calculus Functions I

M	A	T	H	O

Directions: Using a pen fill in your card with a random assignment of the numbers from 1-30. You will use only 25 of the 30 numbers. Do not use a number more than once. You will need pencil and paper to work out your answers. Any 5 in a row wins!

1. $\dfrac{-1}{2}\cos x + c$	7. $\dfrac{-1}{2}x^{-2} + \dfrac{2}{3}x^{\frac{3}{2}} - \dfrac{12}{5}x^{\frac{5}{4}} + c$	13. $\dfrac{1}{3}x^3 + \dfrac{3}{2}x^2 - \dfrac{2}{3}x + c$	19. $\dfrac{2}{3}x^{\frac{3}{2}} + c$	25. $\dfrac{3}{7}x^{\frac{7}{3}} + c$
2. $4\sin x + c$	8. $\dfrac{3}{7}x^7 - \dfrac{3}{5}x^{\frac{5}{3}} - 5x^{\frac{4}{5}} + c$	14. $\dfrac{3}{7}x^7 - \dfrac{2}{3}x^3 + \dfrac{7}{2}x^2 + x + c$	20. $-4\sin x + c$	26. $\dfrac{1}{4}x^4 + x^2 + c$
3. $\dfrac{1}{2}x^2 + \dfrac{1}{3}x^3 + c$	9. $-2\cos x + c$	15. $\dfrac{1}{2}x^2 - 2x^{-1} + \dfrac{1}{3}x^{-3} + c$	21. $\dfrac{1}{2}\sin x + c$	27. $\dfrac{1}{4}x^4 - x^2 + 7x + c$
4. $\dfrac{-1}{4}x^{-2} + c$	10. $\dfrac{-1}{4}\cos x + c$	16. $4x + \dfrac{4}{3}x^3 + \dfrac{1}{5}x^5 + c$	22. $\dfrac{1}{4}\sin x + c$	28. $\dfrac{1}{2}x^2 + \dfrac{1}{5}x^5 + c$
5. $\dfrac{-1}{x} - 2x + c$	11. $\dfrac{-1}{4x^4} + c$	17. $2x^4 - 4x^{\frac{3}{2}} - \dfrac{1}{x} + c$	23. $\dfrac{-1}{2}\sin x + c$	29. $\dfrac{-1}{2}x^{-2} - 2x + c$
6. $\dfrac{1}{3}x^3 + c$	12. $2\cos x + c$	18. $\dfrac{2}{3}x^{\frac{3}{2}} + 2x^3 + c$	24. $\dfrac{3}{5}x^{\frac{5}{3}} + c$	30. $x^7 + \dfrac{4}{3}x^{\frac{3}{2}} + c$

Integrating Calculus Functions I

Problem:	Answer:		Problem:	Answer:
1. $\int x^2 dx$	6		17. $\int x(1+x^3)dx$	28
2. $\int (8x^3 - 6x^{\frac{1}{2}} + x^{-2})dx$	17		18. $\int \dfrac{1-2x^3}{x^3}dx$	29
3. $\int (x^3 + 2x)dx$	26		19. $\int (-2\sin x)dx$	12
4. $\int \dfrac{dx}{x^5}$	11		20. $\int (-4\cos x)dx$	20
5. $\int (\sqrt{x})dx$	19		21. $\int (2\sin x)dx$	9
6. $\int (x + x^2)dx$	3		22. $\int \dfrac{x^5 + 2x^2 - 1}{x^4}dx$	15
7. $\int (3x^6 - 2x^2 + 7x + 1)dx$	14		23. $\int (\sqrt{x} + 6x^2)dx$	18
8. $\int (4\cos x)dx$	2		24. $\int (x^2 + 3x - \frac{2}{3})dx$	13
9. $\int \dfrac{x^2 - 2x^4}{x^4}dx$	5		25. $\int (\frac{1}{2}\sin x)dx$	1
10. $\int \sqrt[3]{x^2}dx$	24		26. $\int (\frac{1}{2}\cos x)dx$	21
11. $\dfrac{1}{2x^3}dx$	4		27. $\int (\frac{1}{4}\sin x)dx$	10
12. $\int x\left(\sqrt[3]{x}\right)dx$	25		28. $\int (\frac{1}{4}\cos x)dx$	22
13. $\int (x^3 - 2x + 7)dx$	27		29. $\int (\frac{-1}{2}\cos x)dx$	23
14. $\int (x^{-3} + \sqrt{x} - 3x^{\frac{1}{4}})dx$	7		30. $\int (7x^6 + 2x^{\frac{1}{2}})dx$	30
15. $\int (3x^6 - x^{\frac{2}{3}} - 4x^{\frac{-1}{5}})dx$	8			
16. $\int (4 + 4x^2 + x^4)dx$	16			

Integrating Calculus Functions II

M	A	T	H	O

Directions: Using a pen fill in your card with a random assignment of the numbers from 1-30. You will use only 25 of the 30 numbers. Do not use a number more than once. You will need pencil and paper to work out your answers. Any 5 in a row wins!

1. $x^3 + 2x^2 + c$	**7.** $\dfrac{-5}{2}e^{x^2+2} + c$	**13.** $(2+x^2)^{\frac{3}{2}} + c$	**19.** $\dfrac{1}{3}(2x)^{\frac{3}{2}} + c$	**25.** $\dfrac{1}{3}\sin^3 x + c$
2. $\dfrac{1}{3}(3x^2+7)^{\frac{3}{2}} + c$	**8.** $\sin(x^2+3x) + c$	**14.** $\ln|\ln x| + c$	**20.** $x^2 - \cos x + c$	**26.** $\dfrac{-1}{3}\cos^3 x + c$
3. $\dfrac{-1}{x} + c$	**9.** $2e^{1+3x} + c$	**15.** $\dfrac{-3}{2}\sin 2x + c$	**21.** $\dfrac{1}{2}(\ln x)^2 + c$	**27.** $2x + \dfrac{1}{3}x^3 + c$
4. $\dfrac{1}{2}(e^{2x}) + c$	**10.** $\dfrac{1}{10}(x^2+1)^5 + c$	**16.** $-2\ln(x^2+1) + c$	**22.** $-2\cos x + c$	**28.** $\dfrac{1}{5}x^5 + \dfrac{2}{3}x^3 + x + c$
5. $\dfrac{1}{5}(x-1)^5 + c$	**11.** $\dfrac{1}{2}\sin 2x + c$	**17.** $\dfrac{-2}{5}(x^2+1)^5 + c$	**23.** $2(x-1)^{\frac{1}{2}} + c$	**29.** $\dfrac{1}{2}e^{x^2+2} + c$
6. $\dfrac{1}{6}(3x^2+7)^3 + c$	**12.** $\dfrac{1}{5}x^5 - x^3 + 5\ln|x| + c$	**18.** $\dfrac{1}{2}\ln(x^2+1) + c$	**24.** $\dfrac{1}{3}(x^2+2)^{\frac{3}{2}} + c$	**30.** $\dfrac{-1}{2}\cos 2x + c$

Integrating Calculus Functions II

Problems:	Answers:		Problems:	Answers:
1. $\int (x-1)^4 dx$	5		16. $\int (x^2+1)^4(-4x)dx$	17
2. $\int x(x^2+1)^4 dx$	10		17. $\int (x^2+1)^2 dx$	28
3. $\int \dfrac{x}{x^2+1}dx$	18		18. $\int 3x\sqrt{3x^2+7}dx$	2
4. $\int 3x\sqrt{2+x^2}dx$	13		19. $\int 2\sin x\, dx$	22
5. $\int \sqrt{2x}dx$	19		20. $\int \cos^2 x \sin x\, dx$	26
6. $\int x\sqrt{x^2+2}dx$	24		21. $\int -3\cos 2x\, dx$	15
7. $\int \dfrac{dx}{\sqrt{x-1}}$	23		22. $\int (x^4-3x^2+\dfrac{5}{x})dx$	12
8. $\int \sin 2x\, dx$	30		23. $\int 3x(3x^2+7)^2 dx$	6
9. $\int \cos 2x\, dx$	11		24. $\int (2x+\sin x)dx$	20
10. $\int \dfrac{\ln x}{x}dx$	21		25. $\int \dfrac{1}{x^2}dx$	3
11. $\int \dfrac{1}{x\ln x}dx$	14		26. $\int e^{2x}dx$	4
12. $\int \dfrac{-4x}{x^2+1}dx$	16		27. $\int -5xe^{x^2+2}dx$	7
13. $\int xe^{x^2+2}dx$	29		28. $\int (2x+3)\cos(x^2+3x)dx$	8
14. $\int (3x^2+4x)dx$	1		29. $\int 6e^{1+3x}dx$	9
15. $\int \sin^2 x \cos x\, dx$	25		30. $\int (2+x^2)dx$	27

Section 2:

Square

Puzzles

Evaluating Expressions
Square Puzzle

Directions: Cut out the squares below. Rearrange these squares back into a 4x4 grid by working a given problem, finding the answer (simplified fully) on a square, and placing the problem and answer on adjacent edges. When all problems have been completed, if your work is correct, then the pieces will fit perfectly to re-form a 4x4 grid. Paste or tape your completed puzzle to a piece of paper.

To solve, substitute: $a = 1, b = 3, c = -4, x = \dfrac{1}{2}, y = 10, z = -2$

top: czx left: $b+c$ right: $\frac{1}{2}by$ bottom: x	top: $cz-bxy$ left: b^2 right: $xz-c$ bottom: bc	top: $-y$ left: $a+b+c$ right: $b-a$	top: $c+b$ right: $y-z+bc$
top: c^2+bz left: $\frac{-by}{z}$ right: $-a$ bottom: $c-b$	top: xy right: b^2-z bottom: $cx+a$	right: $x(y-z)$ bottom: xc^2	top: $\frac{z}{c}$ left: $\frac{y^2-a}{b^2}$ right: $b(a-z)$ bottom: $bc-z$
top: $y-b$ left: -c	left: $2b$ right: $\frac{yz+c}{cz}$ bottom: $|c|$	left: $2ax$ bottom: $2c+z+y$	top: cz right: $\frac{y+z}{2c}$ bottom: $-(a+c+z)$
left: $-|c+a|$ right: a^2 bottom: b^2-c-b	top: $-|z|$ left: $xy+z$ bottom: $b+|c|$	top: $z-y$ left: $8x^2$ right: z^2	top: $y+5z$ left: b^2-y bottom: cx

73

Evaluating Expressions
Square Puzzle
ANSWER KEY

$x(y-z)$ $\quad$ xc^2	$2b$ $\quad$ $|c|$	$\dfrac{yz+c}{cz}$	$-\lvert c+a \rvert$ $\quad a^2$ $\quad b^2-c-b$	$2ax$ $\quad 2c+z+y$
cz $\quad$ $\dfrac{y+z}{2c}$ $\quad -(a+c+z)$	czx $\quad b+c$ $\quad x$	c^2+bz $\quad \dfrac{1}{2}by$ $\quad \dfrac{-by}{z}$ $\quad c-b$	$y+5z$ $\quad b^2-y$ $\quad cx$
xy $\quad b^2-z$ $\quad cx+a$	$\dfrac{z}{c}$ $\quad \dfrac{y^2-a}{b^2}$ $\quad b(a-z)$ $\quad bc-z$	$cz-bxy$ $\quad b^2$ $\quad xz-c$ $\quad bc$	$-\lvert z \rvert$ $\quad xy+z$ $\quad b+\lvert c \rvert$
$c+b$ $\quad y-z+bc$	$-y$ $\quad a+b+c$ $\quad b-a$	$z-y$ $\quad 8x^2$ $\quad z^2$	$y-b$ $\quad$ -c

Equation Solving
Square Puzzle

Directions: Cut out the squares below. Rearrange these squares back into a 4x4 grid by working a given problem, finding the answer (simplified fully) on a square, and placing the problem and answer on adjacent edges. When all problems have been completed, if your work is correct, then the pieces will fit perfectly to re-form a 4x4 grid. Paste or tape your completed puzzle to a piece of paper.

Row 1

Cell (1,1)	Cell (1,2)	Cell (1,3)	Cell (1,4)
top: $\frac{13}{2}$; right: $-3(2-3x)=9$; bottom: 2	top: 2; left: no solution; bottom: 10	bottom: $2x-5=8$; right: $-2(x+4)+5=1$	top: $\frac{9}{2}$; left: $\underline{6}$; right: $3(4-x)+5x=9$; bottom: -3

Row 2

Cell (2,1)	Cell (2,2)	Cell (2,3)	Cell (2,4)
top: $-2-x=-12$; left: -21	left: $12+(x+9)=7$; bottom: 0; right: $5x+6=2x+3-x$	top: $-4x+5=-3$; bottom: $6-3x=18$; right: $3(x-2)=12$	top: $-18+18x=-18$; left: $\underline{-6}$; bottom: 3; right: -4

Row 3

Cell (3,1)	Cell (3,2)	Cell (3,3)	Cell (3,4)
left: -2; bottom: $-9x+3=15$	top: -4; left: -14; right: $4=7x-20$	left: $-3/4$; bottom: $-x+4=-8$	top: $\frac{-9}{2}$; left: -5; right: $x-3=2x+18$

Row 4

Cell (4,1)	Cell (4,2)	Cell (4,3)	Cell (4,4)
top: $3x-3=-12$; left: $24/7$; right: $4=-2(x+3)$	left: $4-(2x+5)=6x+31$; top: 12; bottom: $15=7x+1$	top: $-3x-3=-12$; left: $-3/2$; bottom: $2x+3=-6$; right: $2(x+2)=4x+1-2x$	top: $\frac{-4}{3}$; left: $5/3$; bottom: $2x-3=6$; right: $-(x+2)=4$

Equation Solving
Square Puzzle
ANSWER KEY

Row 1

$-2(x+4) + 5 = 1$	-2 ... $-9x + 3 = 15$	-14 ... $12 + (x+9) = 7$	$5x + 6 = 2x + 3 - x$ ... $-3/4$
$2x - 5 = 8$		0	$-x + 4 = -8$

Row 2

13	$\dfrac{-4}{3}$	$-18 + 18x = -18$	12
$-3(2 - 3x) = 9$	$5/3$ ... $-(x + 2) = 4$	-6 ... -4	$4 - (2x+5) = 6x+31$
2	$2x - 3 = 6$	3	$15 = 7x + 1$

Row 3

$-4x + 5 = -3$	$\dfrac{9}{2}$	$-3x - 3 = -12$	2
$3(x - 2) = 12$	6	$-3/2$ ... $3(4 - x) + 5x = 9$	$2(x + 2) = 4x + 1 - 2x$ — no solution
$6 - 3x = 18$	-3	$2x + 3 = -6$	10

Row 4

-4	$3x - 3 = -12$	$\dfrac{-9}{2}$	$-2 - x = -12$
$4 = 7x - 20$	$24/7$ ... $4 = -2(x + 3)$	-5 ... $x - 3 = 2x + 18$	-21

Solving Linear Inequalities
Square Puzzle

Directions: Cut out the squares below. Rearrange these squares back into a 4x4 grid by working a given problem, finding the answer (simplified fully) on a square, and placing the problem and answer on adjacent edges. When all problems have been completed, if your work is correct, then the pieces will fit perfectly to re-form a 4x4 grid. Paste or tape your completed puzzle to a piece of paper.

$x > 3/4$ $x - 4 \le 3x + 8$	$3 < 3x + 12$ $x \le -2$ ... $4 + 3x > 4x + 11$ $6x + 2 \le 3x - 10$	$14 \ge -2x$ $x + 3 < 7$	$x < 10$ $8 < 4 - 2x$
$x < 4$ $x - 4 > -3$ $-x + 3 < 8$	$8 - 3x \le 2x + 18$ $x \le -4$ $x \le 4$	$x \ge -6$ $x < -3$ $-x + 4 \le -3x + 6$	$x < -1$ $x \ge -2$
$x \le \dfrac{-1}{6}$ $x < -2$ ... $3x - 3 \le 9$	$x \ge -7$ ... $2(3 - x) + 4x \le -6$ $x > \dfrac{-3}{2}$	$x < -3$ $x \le 5$ ... $-4x \ge 2x + 12$ $4 - 6x \ge 5$	$x > 4$ $x \ge -8$ ... $x + 6 > 9x + 30$ $x > -3$
$x > -5$ $-2x - 4 \le -5x + 11$ $6 > x - 4$	$x \le 1$ $x < -7$ $-3(2x + 4) > 6x$	$x \le -6$ ... $6(3 - x) < 2x + 12$ $14 > -9x + 50$	$-2x < 3$ $x > 1$ ... $2(x-3) \le 4x + 10$ $12x + 24 < -12$

77

Solving Linear Inequalities
Square Puzzle
ANSWER KEY

$x + 3 < 7$ $14 \geq -2x$	$x \geq -7$ $x > \dfrac{-3}{2}$ $2(3 - x) + 4x \leq -6$	$x \leq -6$ $14 > -9x + 50$ $6(x - 3) > 2x + 12$	$x > 3/4$ $x - 4 \leq 3x + 8$
$x < 4$ $x - 4 > -3$ $-x + 3 < 8$	$-2x < 3$ $x > 1$ $2(x-3) \leq 4x + 10$ $12x + 24 < -12$	$x > 4$ $x \geq -8$ $x + 9 > 6x + 30$ $x > -3$	$x \geq -6$ $x < -3$ $-x + 4 \leq -3x + 6$
$x > -5$ $-2x - 4 \leq -5x + 11$ $6 > x - 4$	$x < -3$ $x \leq 5$ $-4x \geq 2x + 12$ $4 - 6x \geq 5$	$3 < 3x + 12$ $x \leq -2$ $3x + 4 < 4x + 11$ $6x + 2 \leq 3x - 10$	$x \leq 1$ $x < -7$ $-3(2x + 4) > 6x$
$x < 10$ $8 < 4 - 2x$	$x \leq \dfrac{-1}{6}$ $x < -2$ $3x - 3 \leq 9$	$x \leq -4$ $x \geq 4$ $8 - 3x \leq 2x + 18$	$x < -1$ $x \geq -2$

Writing Equations of Lines
Square Puzzle

Directions: Cut out the squares below. Rearrange these squares back into a 4x4 grid by working a given problem, finding the answer (simplified fully) on a square, and placing the problem and answer on adjacent edges. When all problems have been completed, if your work is correct, then the pieces will fit perfectly to re-form a 4x4 grid. Paste or tape your completed puzzle to a piece of paper.

Row 1

Cell (1,1):
- bottom: m=4, pt. (2,3)
- right: m=2, pt. (-3,1)

Cell (1,2):
- top: $y = x + 2$
- left: (-1,-2) (0,3)
- right: $y = -2x + 5$
- bottom: $y = 3x + 10$

Cell (1,3):
- top: pts. (10,3) (0,-2)
- left: $y = (-1/2)x + 3/2$
- right: $y = -3x + 3$
- bottom: pts. (1,0) (-2,4)

Cell (1,4):
- top: pts. (-4,6) (4,-6)
- left: $y = (5/2)x$
- right: $y = -3x + 15$

Row 2

Cell (2,1):
- top: $y = -4x - 1$
- left: pts. (4,-3) (3,-6)

Cell (2,2):
- top: $y = x - 3$
- right: pts. (0,0) (2,5)

Cell (2,3):
- top: $y = -2x - 3$
- left: m=0, pt. (1/2, -4)
- bottom: $m = \dfrac{-2}{3}, pt.(-1,-2)$

Cell (2,4):
- top: $y = -x + 6$
- right: m=2, pt. (-4,7)
- bottom: pts. (6,3) (5,2)

Row 3

Cell (3,1):
- left: $y = -x + 5$
- bottom: $m = -2, pt.(-4,5)$

Cell (3,2):
- top: pts.(-4,-2) (-2,4)
- left: $y = 2x + 15$
- bottom: $y = \dfrac{-3}{2}x$

Cell (3,3):
- top: pts. (-2,-2) (-1,-4)
- left: m= -1/2, pt. (1,1)
- right: m=-2, pt.(3,-1)
- bottom: $y = \dfrac{1}{2}x - 2$

Cell (3,4):
- top: $y = \dfrac{-2}{3}x - \dfrac{8}{3}$
- left: $y = -4$
- right: m=-3, pt. (2,-3)
- bottom: pts. (2,-9) (0,-1)

Row 4

Cell (4,1):
- left: $y = -2x + 10$
- right: m=-1, pt. (4,1)
- bottom: $y = -2x - 6$

Cell (4,2):
- left: pts. (4,3) (3,6)
- top: $y = \dfrac{-4}{3}x + \dfrac{4}{3}$
- right: $y = 3x - 15$

Cell (4,3):
- top: $y = 4x - 5$
- right: $y = 5x + 3$
- bottom: m=-1, pt. (6,0)

Cell (4,4):
- left: $y = 2x + 7$
- right: pts. (3,4) (2,6)
- bottom: pts. (4,6) (-1,1)

Writing Equations of Lines
Square Puzzle
ANSWER KEY

m=4, pt. (2,3) m=2, pt. (-3,1)	$y = 2x + 7$ pts. (4,6) (-1,1)	pts. (3,4) (2,6) $y=-2x+10$ $y = -2x - 6$	m=-1, pt. (4,1) $y = -x + 5$ $m = -2, pt.(-4,5)$
$y = 4x - 5$ m=-1, pt. (6,0)	$y = x + 2$ $y= 5x + 3$ (-1,-2) (0,3) $y = 3x +10$	pts. (-2,-2) (-1,-4) m=-2, pt.(3,-1) $y=-2x + 5$ $y = \dfrac{1}{2}x - 2$	$y = -2x - 3$ m=0, pt. (1/2,-4) y=-4 $m = \dfrac{-2}{3}, pt.(-1,-2)$
$y = -x + 6$ pts. (6,3) (5,2)	pts.$(-4,-2)$ $(-2,4)$ m=2, pt. (-4,7) $y = 2x + 15$ $y = \dfrac{-3}{2}x$	pts. (10,3) (0,-2) y=(-1/2)x + 3/2 m= -1/2, pt. (1,1) pts. (1,0) (-2,4)	$y = \dfrac{-2}{3}x - \dfrac{8}{3}$ m=-3, pt. (2,-3) y=-3x + 3 pts. (2,-9) (0,-1)
$y = x - 3$ pts. (0,0) (2,5)	pts. (-4,6) (4,-6) y = (5/2)x y= -3x + 15	$y = \dfrac{-4}{3}x + \dfrac{4}{3}$ pts. (4,3) (3,6) y = 3x – 15	$y = -4x - 1$ pts. (4,-3) (3,-6)

System of Equations
Square Puzzle

Directions: Cut out the squares below. Rearrange these squares back into a 4x4 grid by working a given problem, finding the answer (simplified fully) on a square, and placing the problem and answer on adjacent edges. When all problems have been completed, if your work is correct, then the pieces will fit perfectly to re-form a 4x4 grid. Paste or tape your completed puzzle to a piece of paper.

Row 1

Cell (1,1): top $x-2y=5$, $3x-5y=8$; left $(0,-4)$; right $5x+4y=12$, $3x=4+4y$

Cell (1,2): top $(0,0)$; right $y=3x+5$, $y=x+5$; bottom $2x-y=-4$, $-3x+y=-9$

Cell (1,3): top $(3,-2)$; left $(2,4)$; right $3x-y=4$, $6x+2y=-8$

Cell (1,4): top $(-1,-5)$; left $(3,0)$; $\frac{1}{2}x+\frac{2}{3}y=-3$, $4x-\frac{1}{3}y=-7$

Row 2

Cell (2,1): top $y=-4x+20$, $x-\frac{2}{3}y=\frac{4}{3}$; left $(0,5)$; right $(3,4)$; bottom $y+4x=12$, $3y-4x=8$

Cell (2,2): left $(4,1/3)$; bottom $x+3y=5$, $-x+y=3$

Cell (2,3): top $(-2,-3)$; left $(2,1/2)$

Cell (2,4): left $(4,0)$; right $x-3y=3$, $2x+9y=11$; $y=x-2$, $y=4x+1$

Row 3

Cell (3,1): top $(-1,-3)$; left $3x=13-y$, $2x-y=2$; bottom $(1,2)$

Cell (3,2): top $(3,-4)$; left $3x+y=6$, $4x+y=7$

Cell (3,3): top $(-1,2)$; left $x+y=6$, $y=2x$; right $(1,3)$; $2x+3y=-17$, $y=x-4$

Cell (3,4): top $(\frac{7}{4},5)$; left $(4,5/3)$; right $(3,3)$; $y=x-5$, $y=-2x+4$

Row 4

Cell (4,1): left $y-4x=3$, $y=x$; $2x+y=8$, $x-y=4$; bottom $(4,4)$

Cell (4,2): bottom $y=1/2\,x$, $x+2y=0$

Cell (4,3): top $(13,30)$; left $(-1,-1)$; right $4x-3y=11$, $2x+3y=13$; bottom $x=y+7$, $2x+y=2$

Cell (4,4): top $2x-3y=-4$, $x=7-3y$; left $y=x$, $x+y=6$; right $x-y=3$, $y+x=3$; bottom $(-9,-7)$

Solving Systems of Equations
Square Puzzle
ANSWER KEY

$(-1,-1)$ y = 1/2 x x + 2y=0	y − 4x=3 y = x (4,4)	2x+y =8 x − y =4 (4, 0) $y = x - 2$ $y = 4x + 1$	x − 3y =3 2x+9y =11 (4, 1/3) $x + 3y = 5$ $-x + y = 3$
(0,0) $2x - y = -4$ $-3x + y = -9$	$y =3x+5$ $y =x+5$ $y = -4x + 20$ $x - \dfrac{2}{3}y = \dfrac{4}{3}$ (0, 5) $y + 4x = 12$ $3y - 4x = 8$	(−1,−3) 3x =13 − y 2x − y =2 (3, 4) (1,2)	(−1,2) 3x+y=6 4x+y=7 (1, 3) $2x + 3y = -17$ $y = x - 4$
(13,30 $x = y + 7$ $2x + y = 2$ 4x-3y =11 2x+3y =13	(4, 5/3) $(\dfrac{7}{4},5)$ $y = x - 5$ $y = -2x + 4$	$2x - 3y = -4$ $x = 7 - 3v$ (3, 3) y=x x+y=6 x-y =3 y+x =3 (−9,−7)	(−1,−5) (3,0) $\dfrac{1}{2}x + \dfrac{2}{3}y = -3$ $4x - \dfrac{1}{3}y = -7$
(3,−4) x+y=6 y=2x	(3,−2) (2, 4) 3x-y =4 6x+2y =-8	$x - 2y = 5$ $3x - 5y = 8$ (0,-4) 5x+4y=12 3x=4+4y	(-2,-3) (2, 1/2)

82

Multiplication of Monomials
Square Puzzle

Directions: Cut out the squares below. Rearrange these squares back into a 4x4 grid by working a given problem, finding the answer (simplified fully) on a square, and placing the problem and answer on adjacent edges. When all problems have been completed, if your work is correct, then the pieces will fit perfectly to re-form a 4x4 grid. Paste or tape your completed puzzle to a piece of paper.

Row 1:

Cell (1,1) — top: $-27x^3y^{12}$; left: $16x^4$; right: $(6xy^2)(-2x^3y^5)$; bottom: $(-2x^5y^6)^2$

Cell (1,2) — top: $-3x^3y^{12}$; left: $27x^6$; right: $(2x^2)(-4x^3)$; bottom: $(4x^2y)^3$

Cell (1,3) — top: $-x^3y^5$; left: $-6x^3y^2$; right: $(3x^2)^3$; bottom: $(-3xy^4)^3$

Cell (1,4) — right: $x^2(2x^3)$; bottom: $(3x^2y)(4xy^3)(5xy)$

Row 2:

Cell (2,1) — top: x^3y^9; left: $-8x^5$; bottom: $(4x)^2(y^3)$

Cell (2,2) — top: $64x^6y^3$; left: $-12x^4y^7$; right: $(2x^2y)^3$; bottom: $-2x^5(y^6)^2$

Cell (2,3) — left: $2x^5$; right: $(-3x^2)(6x^5)$; bottom: $(-xy^2)(x^2y^3)$

Cell (2,4) — top: $60x^4y^5$; right: $(-3x^2y)(2xy)$; bottom: $(-2x^2)^3$

Row 3:

Cell (3,1) — top: $-8x^6$; right: $(-4x^2)^2$; bottom: $(-5xy)(6x^2y^2)$

Cell (3,2) — left: $9x^6$; bottom: $(xy^3)^3$

Cell (3,3) — top: $16x^2y^3$; left: $8x^6y^3$; bottom: $2(3x)^3$

Cell (3,4) — left: $-18x^7$; right: $(-3x^3)^2$; bottom: $-3(xy^4)^3$

Row 4:

Cell (4,1) — top: $-2x^5y^{12}$; left: $-x^6$; right: $(6x^7)(-3x^9)$

Cell (4,2) — top: $4x^{10}y^{12}$; left: $-6x^5$; bottom: $(-x^2)^3$

Cell (4,3) — top: $54x^3$; left: $-18x^{16}$

Cell (4,4) — top: $-30x^3y^3$; right: $(2x^2)(-3x^3)$

83

Multiplication of Monomials
Square Puzzle
ANSWER KEY

$x^2(2x^3)$ $(3x^2y)(4xy^3)(5xy)$	$2x^5$ $(-xy^2)(x^2y^3)$	$(-3x^2)(6x^5)$ $-18x^7$ $-3(xy^4)^3$	$(-3x^3)^2$ $9x^6$ $(xy^3)^3$
$60x^4y^5$ $(-3x^2y)(2xy)$ $(-2x^2)^3$	$-x^3y^5$ $-6x^3y^2$ $(-3xy^4)^3$	$-3x^3y^{12}$ $(3x^2)^3$ $27x^6$ $(4x^2y)^3$	x^3y^9 $(2x^2)(-4x^3)$ $-8x^5$ $(4x)^2(y^3)$
$-8x^6$ $(-4x^2)^2$ $(-5xy)(6x^2y^2)$	$-27x^3y^{12}$ $16x^4$ $(-2x^5y^6)^2$	$64x^6y^3$ $(6xy^2)(-2x^3y^5)$ $-12x^4y^7$ $-2x^5(y^6)^2$	$16x^2y^3$ $(2x^2y)^3$ $8x^6y^3$ $2(3x)^3$
$-30x^3y^3$ $(2x^2)(-3x^3)$	$4x^{10}y^{12}$ $-6x^5$ $(-x^2)^3$	$-2x^5y^{12}$ $-x^6$ $(6x^7)(-3x^9)$	$54x^3$ $-18x^{16}$

Multiplying Binomials
Square Puzzle

Directions: Cut out the squares below. Rearrange these squares back into a 4x4 grid by working a given problem, finding the answer (simplified fully) on a square, and placing the problem and answer on adjacent edges. When all problems have been completed, if your work is correct, then the pieces will fit perfectly to re-form a 4x4 grid. Paste or tape your completed puzzle to a piece of paper.

right: $8x^2 - 10x + 3$ bottom: $2x^2 + 11x - 21$	top: $(2x-3)(x+8)$ left: $(x+5)(x+3)$ right: $x^2 - 3x - 28$	left: $(3x-4)(2x+3)$ right: $8x^2 + 6x + 1$ bottom: $2x^2 + 5x + 3$	top: $(3x+7)(x-5)$ left: $(x-7)(x+4)$
top: $(3x-1)(x+1)$ right: $6x^2 + 7x - 3$ bottom: $x^2 + 2x + 1$	top: $(3x+4)(x-5)$ left: $(2x+1)(x+3)$ right: $7x^2 - 8x + 1$ bottom: $8x^2 - x - 9$	left: $(4x-3)(2x-1)$ right: $6x^2 + x - 12$ bottom: $3x^2 - 11x - 20$	top: $(x+1)(x+1)$ right: $2x^2 - 17x + 30$
left: $(4x+1)(2x+1)$ bottom: $5x^2 - 16x + 3$	top: $(3x-2)(2x-1)$ left: $(4x-3)(3x+4)$ right: $5x^2 + 13x - 6$ bottom: $2x^2 + 13x - 24$	top: $(2x-3)(x+7)$ right: $2x^2 + 7x + 3$ bottom: $3x^2 + 2x - 1$	top: $(5x-1)(x-3)$ left: $(7x-4)(x-2)$ bottom: $10 + x - 2x^2$
top: $(3x-2)(x+1)$ left: $(2x-5)(x-6)$ right: $x^2 + 8x + 15$	top: $(8x-9)(x+1)$ left: $(3x-1)(2x+3)$ right: $12x^2 + 7x - 12$ bottom: $3x^2 + x - 2$	top: $(2x+3)(x+1)$ left: $(7x-1)(x-1)$ right: $7x^2 - 18x + 8$ bottom: $6x^2 - 7x + 2$	top: $(5-2x)(2+x)$ left: $(5x-2)(x+3)$ bottom: $3x^2 - 8x - 35$

Multiplying Binomials
Square Puzzle
ANSWER KEY

Row 1

$8x^2 - 10x + 3$ (right)	$(4x - 3)(2x - 1)$ (right)	$(3x - 4)(2x + 3)$ (top) · $6x^2 + x - 12$ (right)	$(4x + 1)(2x + 1)$ (top) · $8x^2 + 6x + 1$ (right)
$2x^2 + 11x - 21$ (bottom)	$3x^2 - 11x - 20$ (bottom)	$2x^2 + 5x + 3$ (bottom)	$5x^2 - 16x + 3$ (bottom)

Row 2

$(2x - 3)(x + 7)$ (top) · $2x^2 + 7x + 3$ (right)	$(3x + 4)(x - 5)$ (top) · $(2x + 1)(x + 3)$ (left)	$(2x+3)(x+1)$ (top) · $(7x - 1)(x - 1)$ (left) · $7x^2 - 18x + 8$ (right)	$(5x-1)(x-3)$ (top) · $(7x - 4)(x - 2)$ (left)
$3x^2 + 2x - 1$ (bottom)	$8x^2 - x - 9$ (bottom)	$6x^2 - 7x + 2$ (bottom)	$10 + x - 2x^2$ (bottom)

Row 3

$(3x - 1)(x + 1)$ (top) · $6x^2 + 7x - 3$ (right)	$(8x - 9)(x + 1)$ (top) · $(3x - 1)(2x + 3)$ (left)	$(3x - 2)(2x - 1)$ (top) · $(4x - 3)(3x + 4)$ (left) · $12x^2 + 7x - 12$ (right)	$(5 - 2x)(2 + x)$ (top) · $(5x - 2)(x + 3)$ (left) · $5x^2 + 13x - 6$ (right)
$x^2 + 2x + 1$ (bottom)	$3x^2 + x - 2$ (bottom)	$2x^2 + 13x - 24$ (bottom)	$3x^2 - 8x - 35$ (bottom)

Row 4

$(x + 1)(x + 1)$ (top) · $2x^2 - 17x + 30$ (right)	$(3x - 2)(x + 1)$ (top) · $(2x - 5)(x - 6)$ (left)	$(2x - 3)(x + 8)$ (top) · $(x + 5)(x + 3)$ (left) · $x^2 + 8x + 15$ (right)	$(3x + 7)(x - 5)$ (top) · $(x - 7)(x + 4)$ (left) · $x^2 - 3x - 28$ (right)

Factoring
Square Puzzle

Directions: Cut out the squares below. Rearrange these squares back into a 4x4 grid by working a given problem, finding the answer (simplified fully) on a square, and placing the problem and answer on adjacent edges. When all problems have been completed, if your work is correct, then the pieces will fit perfectly to re-form a 4x4 grid. Paste or tape your completed puzzle to a piece of paper.

Row 1

Cell (1,1): left edge $x^2 - x - 2$; bottom edge $(4x-1)(x+5)$

Cell (1,2): top edge $x^2 - x + \dfrac{1}{4}$; left edge $x^2 - 4x + 4$; right edge $(x+1)(x-1)$; bottom edge $(2x+1)^2$

Cell (1,3): top edge $x^2 - \dfrac{1}{4}$; left edge $4x^2 - 1$; right edge $(x-2)^2$; bottom edge $(3x+4)(2x+1)$

Cell (1,4): top edge $4x^2 - x - 5$; right edge $(x+1)(x+2)$; bottom edge $(2x+1)(3x-2)$

Row 2

Cell (2,1): top edge $4x^2 - 4x + 1$; left edge $2x^2 - 7x + 6$; right edge $(x+2)(x-1)$

Cell (2,2): top edge $4x^2 + 4x + 1$; left edge $x^2 - 2x + 1$; right edge $(6x+5)(4x-3)$; bottom edge $(4x+1)(x+5)$

Cell (2,3): top edge $4x^2 + 19x - 5$; left edge $x^2 - 1$; bottom edge $(2x+1)(2x-1)$

Cell (2,4): top edge $x^2 + 4x + 4$; right edge $(x+1)(x-2)$; bottom edge $\left(x-\dfrac{1}{2}\right)^2$

Row 3

Cell (3,1): top edge $x^2 + x + \dfrac{1}{4}$; right edge $(2x+1)(2x-1)$; bottom edge $(4x-5)(x+1)$

Cell (3,2): top edge $4x^2 - 1$; left edge $24x^2 + 2x - 15$; bottom edge $(4x-1)(x-5)$

Cell (3,3): top edge $x^2 + 2x + 1$; right edge $(x+2)^2$; bottom edge $\left(x+\dfrac{1}{2}\right)\left(x-\dfrac{1}{2}\right)$

Cell (3,4): top edge $6x^2 - x - 2$; right edge $(2x-3)(x-2)$

Row 4

Cell (4,1): top edge $4x^2 - 21x + 5$; left edge $x^2 + 4x - 12$

Cell (4,2): right edge $(x+1)^2$; bottom edge $\left(x+\dfrac{1}{2}\right)^2$

Cell (4,3): top edge $6x^2 + 11x + 4$; left edge $x^2 + 3x + 2$; bottom edge $(2x-1)^2$

Cell (4,4): top edge $4x^2 + 21x + 5$; left edge $x^2 + x - 2$; right edge $(x+6)(x-2)$

Factoring
Square Puzzle
ANSWER KEY

$(x+\frac{1}{2})^2$ $(x+1)^2$	x^2+2x+1 $(x+\frac{1}{2})(x-\frac{1}{2})$ $(x+2)^2$	x^2+4x+4 $(x-\frac{1}{2})^2$	$(x+1)(x-2)$ x^2-x-2 $(4x-1)(x+5)$
$x^2+x+\frac{1}{4}$ $(2x+1)(2x-1)$ $(4x-5)(x+1)$	$x^2-\frac{1}{4}$ $4x^2-1$ $(x-2)^2$ $(3x+4)(2x+1)$	$x^2-x+\frac{1}{4}$ x^2-4x+4 $(x+1)(x-1)$ $(2x+1)^2$	$4x^2+19x-5$ x^2-1 $(2x+1)(2x-1)$
$4x^2-x-5$ $(x+1)(x+2)$ $(2x+1)(3x-2)$	$6x^2+11x+4$ x^2+3x+2 $(x-1)^2$ $(2x-1)^2$	$4x^2+4x+1$ x^2-2x+1 $(6x+5)(4x-3)$ $(4x+1)(x+5)$	$4x^2-1$ $24x^2+2x-15$ $(4x-1)(x-5)$
$6x^2-x-2$ $(2x-3)(x-2)$ $2x^2-7x+6$	$4x^2-4x+1$ $(x+2)(x-1)$	$4x^2+21x+5$ x^2+x-2 $(x+6)(x-2)$	$4x^2-21x+5$ $x^2+4x-12$

Multiplication of Radicals
Square Puzzle

Directions: Cut out the squares below. Rearrange these squares back into a 4x4 grid by working a given problem, finding the answer (simplified fully) on a square, and placing the problem and answer on adjacent edges. When all problems have been completed, if your work is correct, then the pieces will fit perfectly to re-form a 4x4 grid. Paste or tape your completed puzzle to a piece of paper.

Row 1

Cell (1,1): right edge: $\sqrt{7} \cdot \sqrt{7}$; bottom edge: $(2+\sqrt{7})(2-\sqrt{7})$

Cell (1,2): top edge: $\sqrt{10}$; left edge: $20 + 10\sqrt{10}$; bottom edge: $3 \cdot 10\sqrt{5}$; right edge: $(3+\sqrt{6})(2-\sqrt{6})$

Cell (1,3): top edge: 6; left edge: $10 + 14\sqrt{3}$; right edge: $(3+\sqrt{5})(4-\sqrt{5})$

Cell (1,4): top edge: $12\sqrt{6}$; left edge: 8; right edge: $2(5+7\sqrt{3})$

Row 2

Cell (2,1): top edge: $10 + 4\sqrt{6}$; right edge: $\sqrt{8} \cdot \sqrt{8}$

Cell (2,2): top edge: $30\sqrt{5}$; left edge: $9 + \sqrt{3}$; bottom edge: $6\sqrt{3} \cdot 2\sqrt{2}$; right edge: $(4+\sqrt{3})(3+\sqrt{3})$

Cell (2,3): top edge: $4 - \sqrt{2}$; left edge: $-\sqrt{6}$; bottom edge: $(1+\sqrt{5})^2$; right edge: $\sqrt{2} \cdot \sqrt{3}$

Cell (2,4): top edge: $12 + 18\sqrt{2}$; left edge: $8 + 3\sqrt{2}$; bottom edge: $\sqrt{3}(1+3\sqrt{2})$

Row 3

Cell (3,1): left edge: 7; right edge: $3\sqrt{6} \cdot 2\sqrt{3}$; bottom edge: $\sqrt{5} \cdot \sqrt{2}$

Cell (3,2): top edge: $\sqrt{3} + 3\sqrt{6}$; left edge: $7 + \sqrt{5}$

Cell (3,3): top edge: -3; left edge: $5(2\sqrt{10}+4)$; bottom edge: $(1-\sqrt{5})(2+\sqrt{5})$

Cell (3,4): left edge: $24\sqrt{6}$; bottom edge: $(3\sqrt{5}-3\sqrt{2})^2$

Row 4

Cell (4,1): top edge: $-3 - \sqrt{5}$; right edge: $(4-\sqrt{3})(3+\sqrt{3})$; bottom edge: $(2+\sqrt{6})^2$

Cell (4,2): top edge: $63 - 18\sqrt{10}$; left edge: $\sqrt{6}$; bottom edge: $6(2+3\sqrt{2})$

Cell (4,3): left edge: $18\sqrt{2}$; right edge: $8 \cdot 3\sqrt{6}$; bottom edge: $(3+\sqrt{2})(2-\sqrt{2})$

Cell (4,4): top edge: $6 + 2\sqrt{5}$; left edge: $15 + 7\sqrt{3}$; right edge: $(2+\sqrt{2})(5-\sqrt{2})$; bottom edge: $(3+\sqrt{3})(3-\sqrt{3})$

Multiplication of Radicals
Square Puzzle
ANSWER KEY

$(2+\sqrt{7})(2-\sqrt{7})$ $\sqrt{7} \bullet \sqrt{7}$	7 $\sqrt{5} \bullet \sqrt{2}$	$3\sqrt{6} \bullet 2\sqrt{3}$ $18\sqrt{2}$ $(3+\sqrt{2})(2-\sqrt{2})$	$8 \bullet 3\sqrt{6}$ $24\sqrt{6}$ $(3\sqrt{5}-3\sqrt{2})^2$
-3 $5(2\sqrt{10}+4)$ $(1-\sqrt{5})(2+\sqrt{5})$	$\sqrt{10}$ $20+10\sqrt{10}$ $3 \bullet 10\sqrt{5}$	$4-\sqrt{2}$ $(3+\sqrt{6})(2-\sqrt{6})$ $-\sqrt{6}$ $(1+\sqrt{5})^2$	$63-18\sqrt{10}$ $\sqrt{2} \bullet \sqrt{3}$ $\sqrt{6}$ $6(2+3\sqrt{2})$
$-3-\sqrt{5}$ $(4-\sqrt{3})(3+\sqrt{3})$ $9+\sqrt{3}$ $(2+\sqrt{6})^2$	$30\sqrt{5}$ $(4+\sqrt{3})(3+\sqrt{3})$ $6\sqrt{3} \bullet 2\sqrt{2}$	$6+2\sqrt{5}$ $15+7\sqrt{3}$ $(2+\sqrt{2})(5-\sqrt{2})$ $(3+\sqrt{3})(3-\sqrt{3})$	$2+18\sqrt{2}$ $8+3\sqrt{2}$ $\sqrt{3}(1+3\sqrt{2})$
$10+4\sqrt{6}$ $\sqrt{8} \bullet \sqrt{8}$	$12\sqrt{6}$ 8 $2(5+7\sqrt{3})$	$10+14\sqrt{3}$ 6 $(3+\sqrt{5})(4-\sqrt{5})$	$\sqrt{3}+3\sqrt{6}$ $7+\sqrt{5}$

90

Identifying Right (or not) Triangles w/the Pythagorean Theorem
Square Puzzle

Directions: Cut out the squares below. Rearrange these squares back into a 4x4 grid by working a given problem, finding the answer (simplified fully) on a square, and placing the problem and answer on adjacent edges. When all problems have been completed, if your work is correct, the pieces will fit perfectly to re-form a 4x4 grid. Paste or tape your completed puzzle to paper. Figures are NOT drawn to scale.

6 c 9 c=? a=3, b=4, c=5	not a right triangle right triangle 8 10 b=? a=5. b=8. c=9	not a right triangle √65 c 9 c=? a=15, b=20, c=25	5√5 a=16, b=30, c=34 √105
right triangle 6 a=7, b=15, c=17	right triangle 6 4 c c=? a=4. b=5. c=6	12 c=? c 5 9 c=?	11 a=7, b=24, c=25 c 6 6 c=?
not a right triangle a=9, b=12, c=15 7 4 c c=? 6 c 10 c=?	√51 right triangle 4√5	9√2 a=? a 11 4 √106	6√2 right triangle b 13 5 b=?
8 b 61 60 b=?	2√13 17 16 a a=? a=3, b=3, c=3√2	3√13 10 b 7 b=? a=10, b=24, c=26	b=? b 12 8 right triangle

91

Identifying Right (or not) Triangles w/the Pythagorean Theorem
Square Puzzle
ANSWER KEY

Row 1:
- Triangle: 6, c, 9, c=?
- a=3, b=4, c=5 | right triangle | Triangle: 6, c, 4, c=?
- a=4, b=5, c=6 | 2√13 | Triangle: 17, a, 15, a=?
- a=3, b=3, c=3√2 | 8 | Triangle: b, 61, 60, b=?

Row 2:
- 3√13 | Triangle: b, 10, 7, b=?
- a=10, b=24, c=26 | not a right triangle | Triangle: 8, 10, b, b=?
- a=5, b=8, c=9 | right triangle | 6 | right triangle | a=7, b=24, c=25
- 11 | Triangle: 6, c, 6, c=?

Row 3:
- √51 | right triangle | 4√5
- a=9, b=12, c=15 | not a right triangle | Triangle: 7, c, 4, 5, c, 10, c=?
- not a right triangle | √65 | Triangle: 9, c, 9, c=?
- a=15, b=20, c=25 | right triangle | 6√2 | Triangle: b, 13, 5, b=?

Row 4:
- b=? | Triangle: b, 12, 8 | right triangle
- a=16, b=30, c=34 | 5√5 | Triangle: a=?, a, 11, 4
- 9√2 | √105 | √106 | Triangle: c=?, c, 5, 9
- 12

92

Composition of Functions
Square Puzzle

Directions: Cut out the squares below. Rearrange these squares back into a 4x4 grid by working a given problem, finding the answer (simplified fully) on a square, and placing the problem and answer on adjacent edges. When all problems have been completed, if your work is correct, then the pieces will fit perfectly to re-form a 4x4 grid. Paste or tape your completed puzzle to a piece of paper.

Use the following functions: $f(x)=3x-5$ $g(x)=x^2-x-7$ $h(x)=\dfrac{5}{x-2}$

23 · right edge: -26	left: g(-3) · right: 1 · bottom: 9h(7)− g(-3)	**$\dfrac{5}{4}$** · right: 6 · bottom: g(f(0))	**0** · left: f(19/3) · bottom: h(f(5))
-1 · left: f(g(0)) · right: -5/8	right: -5/2 · bottom: f(1) + g(2)+h(3)	left: f(2) · bottom: f(h(5))	**$\dfrac{5}{8}$** · left: f(5) • g(4) · bottom: $f(2)\cdot g(7)\cdot h(9)$
left: 25 · bottom: $\dfrac{1}{f(\frac{11}{6})}$	**$\dfrac{-5}{3}$** · left: f(2) +g(-3) · bottom: $\dfrac{f(0)}{g(-3)}$	**4** · left: 2h(0) · right: -35 · bottom: f-3) + g(-3)	**2** · left: 14 · right: -19 · bottom: $\dfrac{h(3)}{f(-1)}$
left: h(0) · right: 5 · bottom: g(h(3))	**13** · left: 3g(0) · right: -5 · bottom: h(g(3))	**-9** · left: -g(7) · bottom: 2g(0) − 3h(5)	**-2** · left: 50 · right: -21 · bottom: $\dfrac{1}{2}h(4)$

93

Composition of Functions
Square Puzzle
ANSWER KEY

-5/2 f(1) + g(2)+ h(3)	h(0) g(h(3))	5 g(-3) 9h(7) − g(-3)	1 f(2) f(h(5))
-2 -21 $\frac{1}{2}h(4)$	13 3g(0) h(g(3))	4 -5 2h(0) f-3) + g(-3)	0 14 f(19/3) h(f(5))
$\frac{5}{4}$ 6 f(2) +g(-3) g(f(0))	$\frac{-5}{3}$ -35 $\frac{f(0)}{g(-3)}$	$\frac{-9}{}$ -g(7) 2g(0) − 3h(5)	$\frac{5}{8}$ 50 f(5) • g(4) $f(2) \bullet g(7) \bullet h(9)$
23 -26	-1 f(g(0))	-19 -5/8 h(3) / f(-1)	25 2 1/ f(11/6)

94

Converting Degree ⟷ Radian Measure
Square Puzzle

Directions: Cut out the squares below. Rearrange these squares back into a 4x4 grid by working a given problem, finding the answer (simplified fully) on a square, and placing the problem and answer on adjacent edges. When all problems have been completed, if your work is correct, then the pieces will fit perfectly to re-form a 4x4 grid. Paste or tape your completed puzzle to a piece of paper.

360^0 350^0 $\qquad$ 180^0	80^0 315^0 $\dfrac{\pi}{6}$	240^0 $\qquad$ $\dfrac{\pi}{2}$ $\dfrac{5\pi}{4}$	210^0 $\dfrac{13\pi}{9}$ $\dfrac{\pi}{4}$
45^0 $\qquad$ 110^0 $\dfrac{3\pi}{4}$	270^0 $\dfrac{11\pi}{18}$ $\qquad$ $\dfrac{\pi}{3}$ 2π	$\dfrac{4\pi}{3}$ $\dfrac{7\pi}{6}$	90^0 $\qquad$ 120^0 $\dfrac{\pi}{18}$
300^0 20^0 $\dfrac{4\pi}{9}$	35^0 π $\qquad$ 0^0	30^0 0	$\dfrac{2\pi}{3}$ $\dfrac{5\pi}{3}$
225^0 260^0 $\qquad$ $\dfrac{11\pi}{6}$ $\dfrac{3\pi}{2}$	10^0 330^0 $\qquad$ $\dfrac{\pi}{9}$ $\dfrac{5\pi}{6}$	135^0 $\dfrac{35\pi}{18}$	150^0 $\dfrac{7\pi}{4}$ $\dfrac{7\pi}{36}$

Converting Degree ⟷ Radian Measure
Square Puzzle
ANSWER KEY

$\dfrac{4\pi}{3}$	240^0 $\dfrac{\pi}{2}$	90^0 120^0	$\dfrac{2\pi}{3}$
$\dfrac{7\pi}{6}$ 210^0	$\dfrac{5\pi}{4}$ 225^0	$\dfrac{\pi}{18}$ 10^0	$\dfrac{5\pi}{3}$ 300^0
$\dfrac{13\pi}{9}$	260^0 $\dfrac{11\pi}{6}$	330^0 $\dfrac{\pi}{9}$	20^0
$\dfrac{\pi}{4}$ 45^0	$\dfrac{3\pi}{2}$ 270^0	$\dfrac{5\pi}{6}$ 150^0	$\dfrac{4\pi}{9}$ 80^0
110^0	$\dfrac{11\pi}{18}$ $\dfrac{\pi}{3}$	$\dfrac{7\pi}{4}$	315^0
$\dfrac{3\pi}{4}$ 135^0	2π 360^0	$\dfrac{7\pi}{36}$ 35^0	$\dfrac{\pi}{6}$ 30^0
$\dfrac{35\pi}{18}$	350^0 180^0	π 0^0	0

Evaluating Trigonometric Values I
Square Puzzle

Directions: Cut out the squares below. Rearrange these squares back into a 4x4 grid by working a given problem, finding the answer (simplified fully) on a square, and placing the problem and answer on adjacent edges. When all problems have been completed, if your work is correct, then the pieces will fit perfectly to re-form a 4x4 grid. Paste or tape your completed puzzle to a piece of paper.

top: $\cos\dfrac{5\pi}{3}$ left: -√3/2 bottom: $\cos\dfrac{\pi}{2}$	top: $\sin\dfrac{3\pi}{2}$ left: sin 5π/4 right: sin π/3 bottom: $\dfrac{-\sqrt{3}}{2}$	top: $\dfrac{-\sqrt{3}}{2}$ left: -1/2 right: √2/2 bottom: -1	top: $\dfrac{\sqrt{2}}{2}$ left: √3/2 right: sin 4π/3 bottom: $\sin\dfrac{5\pi}{6}$
top: $\cos\pi$ left: sin π/4 right: cos 3π/2 bottom: $\sin\dfrac{3\pi}{4}$	top: $\sin\dfrac{5\pi}{6}$ left: 0 bottom: $\dfrac{1}{2}$	left: cos π/3 right: √3/2 bottom: -1	top: cos π/6 right: $\dfrac{1}{2}$
top: $\cos\dfrac{7\pi}{6}$ left: -√2/2 right: cos 3π/4	top: 0 left: √2/2	top: $\sin\dfrac{7\pi}{6}$ right: cos 4π/3 bottom: $\dfrac{-\sqrt{2}}{2}$	top: $\dfrac{1}{2}$ left: -√2/2 right: cos 7π/4
left: sin π right: 1/2 bottom: $\sin\dfrac{5\pi}{3}$	top: 0 bottom: $\dfrac{-1}{2}$	top: $\dfrac{\sqrt{3}}{2}$ right: sin 7π/4	top: $\cos\dfrac{5\pi}{4}$ left: sin 2π/3 bottom: -√2/2

Evaluating Trigonometric Values I
Square Puzzle
ANSWER KEY

0 $\dfrac{-1}{2}$	$\sin \pi$ $\sqrt{2}$ $\sin \dfrac{5\pi}{3}$	$\cos \pi/3$ $\sqrt{3}/2$ -1	$\cos \pi/6$ $\dfrac{1}{2}$
$\sin \dfrac{7\pi}{6}$ cos $4\pi/3$ $\dfrac{-\sqrt{2}}{2}$	$\dfrac{-\sqrt{3}}{2}$ $-1/2$ $\sqrt{2}/2$ -1	$\cos \pi$ $\sin \pi/4$ $\sin \dfrac{3\pi}{4}$	$\sin \dfrac{5\pi}{6}$ cos $3\pi/2$ 0 $\dfrac{1}{2}$
$\cos \dfrac{5\pi}{4}$ $-\sqrt{2}/2$ $\sin \dfrac{2\pi}{3}$	$\sin \dfrac{3\pi}{2}$ sin 5π/4 $\dfrac{-\sqrt{3}}{2}$	sin $\pi/3$ $\dfrac{\sqrt{2}}{2}$ $\sqrt{3}/2$ $\sin \dfrac{5\pi}{6}$	$\cos \dfrac{5\pi}{3}$ sin $4\pi/3$ $-\sqrt{3}/2$ $\cos \dfrac{\pi}{2}$
$\dfrac{\sqrt{3}}{2}$ sin 7π/4	$\cos \dfrac{7\pi}{6}$ $-\sqrt{2}/2$ cos 3π/4	$\dfrac{1}{2}$ $-\sqrt{2}/2$ cos 7π/4	0 $\sqrt{2}/2$

98

Evaluating Trigonometric Values II
Square Puzzle

Directions: Cut out the squares below. Rearrange these squares back into a 4x4 grid by working a given problem, finding the answer (simplified fully) on a square, and placing the problem and answer on adjacent edges. When all problems have been completed, if your work is correct, then the pieces will fit perfectly to re-form a 4x4 grid. Paste or tape your completed puzzle to a piece of paper.

Row 1:

Square (1,1)	Square (1,2)	Square (1,3)	Square (1,4)
left: $\cos 120^0$; bottom: $\sin 90^0$	left: $\cos 300^0$; right: $\sin 210^0$; bottom: $\dfrac{\sqrt{2}}{2}$	top: $\cos 45^0$; left: $1/2$; right: 0; bottom: $\dfrac{\sqrt{2}}{2}$	left: $-1/2$; right: $-1/2$; bottom: $\dfrac{-\sqrt{3}}{2}$

Row 2:

Square (2,1)	Square (2,2)	Square (2,3)	Square (2,4)
top: $\sin 240^0$; left: $\cos 90^0$; right: $\sqrt{2}/2$; bottom: $\dfrac{\sqrt{3}}{2}$	top: 1; left: $\sin 120^0$; right: -1	top: $\dfrac{\sqrt{2}}{2}$; left: $\sqrt{3}/2$; bottom: $\sin 330^0$	top: $\cos 30^0$; left: $-\sqrt{2}/2$; right: $\sin 60^0$; bottom: $\cos 150^0$

Row 3:

Square (3,1)	Square (3,2)	Square (3,3)	Square (3,4)
top: $\sin 150^0$; right: $\sqrt{3}/2$	top: 1; left: $\cos 315^0$; bottom: $\sin 135^0$	right: $1/2$; bottom: $\sin 30^0$	top: $\sin 45^0$; left: $-\sqrt{3}/2$; right: $\cos 225^0$; bottom: $\cos 0^0$

Row 4:

Square (4,1)	Square (4,2)	Square (4,3)	Square (4,4)
top: $\dfrac{-\sqrt{3}}{2}$; left: $\cos 180^0$; right: $\sin 225^0$	top: $\dfrac{1}{2}$; right: $\cos 60^0$; bottom: $\sin 270^0$	top: $\dfrac{-1}{2}$; left: $-\sqrt{2}/2$	top: -1; right: $\sin 300^0$; bottom: $\dfrac{1}{2}$

Evaluating Trigonometric Values II
Square Puzzle
ANSWER KEY

$\frac{1}{2}$ $\sin 30^0$	$\cos 300^0$ $\frac{\sqrt{2}}{2}$ $\sin 210^0$	$-\frac{1}{2}$ $\frac{-\sqrt{3}}{2}$ $-\frac{1}{2}$	$\cos 120^0$ $\sin 90^0$
$\frac{1}{2}$ $\cos 60^0$ $\sin 270^0$	$\cos 45^0$ $\frac{1}{2}$ $\frac{\sqrt{2}}{2}$ 0	$\sin 240^0$ $\cos 90^0$ $\frac{\sqrt{3}}{2}$ $\sqrt{2}/2$	1 $\cos 315^0$ $\sin 135^0$
-1 $\sin 300^0$ $\frac{1}{2}$	$\sin 45^0$ $-\sqrt{3}/2$ $\cos 0^0$ $\cos 225^0$	$\cos 30^0$ $-\sqrt{2}/2$ $\sin 60^0$ $\cos 150^0$	$\frac{\sqrt{2}}{2}$ $\sqrt{3}/2$ $\sin 330^0$
$\sin 150^0$ $\sqrt{3}/2$	1 $\sin 120^0$ -1	$\frac{-\sqrt{3}}{2}$ $\cos 180^0$ $\sin 225^0$	$\frac{-1}{2}$ $-\sqrt{2}/2$

Section 3:

Card Games
&
Other Game
Formats

Baseball Game Directions for Review of Skills

Directions:

This is a game that can be used to review for a test or to practice a specific concept. The teacher can choose 20-30 problems from the text to use for the game but needs to have immediate access to the answer for each problem. The following example shows problems on multiplication and factoring of polynomials.

Have students in the class number off into ones and twos and move their desks onto opposite sides of the room, leaving open space in the middle of the room. Each student will need pencil and paper on which to work. Each team should choose a team name. In the middle of the classroom set up a baseball diamond with the four bases clearly marked.

Flip a coin to see which team will be up to bat first. The teacher will present a problem to be solved. Every student in the room (or pairs on the same team) will need to work the problem to have an answer ready if he or she is the one called upon by the teacher. From the team at bat, the teacher will pick a random student to answer the question. If he or she answers the question correctly, the student will advance to first base and a new question is presented to the class. Everyone again prepares their answer to the question and another random student from the same team is chosen to give their answer. Play continues in this manner with the teacher keeping a record of the runs being scored by each team until a player gives an incorrect answer. Then the same question will be asked of a random student from the team in the field. If that student can give a correct answer, the player from the team at bat is out. Play continues until three outs or five runs are scored by the team at bat. Then the team on the field goes to bat. The game continues until each team has had an equal number of times at bat. Every member of the team with the highest number of runs is awarded three bonus points (or a prize of the teacher's choosing) and every member of the other team is awarded one bonus point (or a lesser prize).

Baseball Game Problems:

Problems:	Answers:	Problems:	Answers:

1. Factor:
$36c^2 - 9d^2$
$(6c + 3d)(6c - 3d)$

2. Factor:
$28r^3s^2 - 14s$
$14s(2r^3s - 1)$

3. Factor:
$2x^2 + x - 6$
$(2x - 3)(x + 2)$

4. Multiply:
$(2x - 5)(5x + 2)$
$10x^2 - 21x - 10$

5. Multiply:
$(4b + 3)^2$
$16b^2 + 24b + 9$

6. Multiply:
$2ab(5a^2 - 7b^2)$
$10a^3b - 14ab^3$

7. Multiply:
$(2y + 1)(y^2 - 2y + 3)$
$2y^3 - 3y^2 + 4y + 3$

8. Factor:
$3x^2 + 3y^2$
$3(x^2 + y^2)$

9. Multiply:
$(4^a - 5)^2$
$16^{a\ 2} - 40^a + 25$

10. Multiply:
$(x - 7)(x + 2)$
$x^2 - 5x - 14$

11. Factor completely:
$ay^2 + 3ay + 2a$
$a(y + 2)(y + 1)$

12. Factor completely:
$a^3 - 4a$
$a(a + 2)(a - 2)$

13. Reduce:
$\dfrac{y^2 - 5y + 6}{y^2 - 4}$
$\dfrac{y - 3}{y + 2}$

14. Reduce:
$\dfrac{4x^2 - 9}{4x + 6}$
$\dfrac{2x - 3}{2}$

15. Factor: $6m^2 + m - 2$ $(3m + 2)(2m - 1)$

16. $\dfrac{6x - 12}{18x - 36}$ $\dfrac{1}{3}$

17. Reduce:
$\dfrac{x^2 - 4}{2 - x}$
$-1(x + 2)$ or $-x - 2$

18. Simplify:
$(y^3 + 2y^2 + 3y - 1) + (3y^2 - 3y^2 - 4y - 2)$
$4y^3 - y^2 - y - 3$

19. Simplify;
$(3x^2 - 5x + 1) - (4x^2 - 3x + 5)$
$x^2 - 2x - 4$

20. Factor:
$10ab - 15a^2b^2$
$5ab(2 - 3ab)$

21. Factor:
$2y - 4y^3$
$2y(1 - 2y^2)$

22. Factor:
$x^2y^2 - 64$
$(xy + 8)(xy - 8)$

23. Factor completely;
$6r^2 - 24s^2$
$6(r + 2s)(r - 2s)$

24. Multiply:
$3x(x^2 - 3y)$
$-3x^3 + 9xy$

25. Factor:
$6f^2 - f - 12$
$(2f - 3)(3f + 4)$

Basketball Shootout Game Directions
For Review of Skills

Directions:

This is a format that can be used to review for a test or to practice a specific concept. The teacher can choose 20-30 problems from the text to use for the game but needs to have immediate access to the answer for each problem.

1. Divide the class into three teams. Each student in the team should pick a partner to work with during the game. They may only talk to their partner while working on a problem, not with other people on their team.

2. The teacher reads a problem or writes it on the board or the overhead, if needed, and allows enough time for all the partner groups to agree on their answer.

3. The teacher randomly calls on a partner group in Team #1 to give their answer.

4. If the answer is correct, Team #1 receives one point and a chance for bonus points by shooting a tennis ball at a trash can placed on a desk against a wall. Masking tape is used to mark a "2 point line" and a "3 point line" on the floor in front of the basket. One try is allowed from the "2 point line" and two tries are allowed from the "3 point line". If the shot is made from the "2 point line", the team gets a total of 2 points, one for getting the question right and one for the shot. If the shot is made from the "3 point line", the team gets a total of 3 points, one for getting the question right and two for the shot. No more than 3 points can be earned on each question.

5. If the answer is incorrect, the same question is asked of a randomly chosen partner group in Team #2, without allowing any extra time to work. If Team #2 gets it right, then they take the shots and earn the points for their team. If they miss the question, then it passes to Team #3 until finally a team is able to answer the question correctly.

6. A new question will be started with the team coming after the one that received the last points, to keep the questions rotating fairly.

7. The team members with the highest number of total points at the end of the game wins a prize such as candy or bonus points on a quiz or test.

Basketball Shootout Game Problems

I. Simplify the following radical fully:

1. $\sqrt{20} = \mathbf{2\sqrt{5}}$
2. $\sqrt{50} = \mathbf{5\sqrt{2}}$
3. $2\sqrt{24} = \mathbf{4\sqrt{6}}$

4. $\sqrt{18} = \mathbf{3\sqrt{2}}$
5. $\sqrt{8} = \mathbf{2\sqrt{2}}$
6. $2\sqrt{20} = \mathbf{4\sqrt{5}}$

7. $\sqrt{27} = \mathbf{3\sqrt{3}}$
8. $2\sqrt{8} = \mathbf{4\sqrt{2}}$
9. $3\sqrt{12} = \mathbf{6\sqrt{3}}$

10. $-5\sqrt{18} = \mathbf{-15\sqrt{2}}$
11. $\sqrt{x^2 y^3} = \mathbf{xy\sqrt{y}}$
12. $\sqrt{20xy^4} = \mathbf{2y^2\sqrt{5x}}$

II. Add or subtract the following radicals:

1. $2\sqrt{7} + 6\sqrt{7} = \mathbf{8\sqrt{7}}$
2. $3\sqrt{5} - 4\sqrt{5} = \mathbf{-\sqrt{5}}$

3. $7\sqrt{6} + \sqrt{6} = \mathbf{8\sqrt{6}}$
4. $-2\sqrt{11} + 15\sqrt{11} = \mathbf{13\sqrt{11}}$

5. $9\sqrt{3} - 5\sqrt{3} = \mathbf{4\sqrt{3}}$
6. $-5\sqrt{5} - 2\sqrt{5} = \mathbf{-7\sqrt{5}}$

7. $2\sqrt{10} - 5\sqrt{10} + \sqrt{10} = \mathbf{-2\sqrt{10}}$
8. $12\sqrt{6} + 5\sqrt{6} + \sqrt{6} = \mathbf{18\sqrt{6}}$

9. $9\sqrt{3} - \sqrt{2} + 9\sqrt{3} = \mathbf{18\sqrt{3} - \sqrt{2}}$
10. $\sqrt{12} - \sqrt{3} = \mathbf{\sqrt{3}}$

11. $3\sqrt{12} + 2\sqrt{3} = \mathbf{8\sqrt{3}}$
12. $5\sqrt{2} - 2\sqrt{8} = \mathbf{\sqrt{2}}$

III. Multiply the following radicals. Make sure your answer is simplified fully.

1. $\sqrt{5} \bullet \sqrt{5} = \mathbf{5}$
2. $\sqrt{3} \bullet \sqrt{2} = \mathbf{\sqrt{6}}$

3. $\sqrt{5} \bullet \sqrt{2} = \mathbf{\sqrt{10}}$
4. $\sqrt{6} \bullet \sqrt{3} = \mathbf{3\sqrt{2}}$

5. $2\sqrt{3} \bullet 3\sqrt{2} = \mathbf{6\sqrt{6}}$
6. $-2\sqrt{5} \bullet 3\sqrt{2} = \mathbf{-6\sqrt{10}}$

7. $3\sqrt{6} \bullet 2\sqrt{2} = \mathbf{12\sqrt{3}}$
8. $\sqrt{2} \bullet 5\sqrt{3} = \mathbf{5\sqrt{6}}$

I Have...Who Has? Card Game Directions

Directions:

Cut out the I Have, Who Has? cards and give one to each student. The teacher will pick a student to begin the game by reading their card aloud. In turn, each student must read his or her card if the answer to the problem read appears on it. The final card read should loop back to the I Have statement on the first card that was read to begin the game.

Optional: The teacher may make a transparency of the cards to display to the class to show students one by one the problems and answers as they are read aloud.

Extensions:

1. Offer a reward like candy or a bonus point to everyone in the class if the game is completed without a mistake.
2. The teacher can time the class during their first round. Have students exchange cards and repeat the activity to beat the class time of the first round.
3. Have teams of students compete against each other to put the cards in order in the fastest time.
4. Cut and paste the cards in a different arrangement to make a set that is not in consecutive order. Make a set of pages for every pair of students. Have students cut apart the cards, put them in order, and glue them onto a sheet of large construction paper.

I have **2x + 5.**
Who has a number 3 less than my number?

I have **2 + 2x.**
Who has a # twice as large as my number?

I have **4x + 4.**
Who has a # 4 less than my number?

I have **4x.**
Who has the square of my #?

I have **16x^2.**
Who has my number increased by 9x^2?

I have **25x^2.**
Who has a square root of my number?

I have **5x.**

Who has twice my number?

I have **10x.**

Who has my number decreased by 9x?

I have **x.**

Who has the square of my #?

I have x^2.

Who has the answer if $-x^2 + 6x$ is added to my #?

I have **6x.**

Who has 6 more than my number?

I have **6x + 6.**

Who has one-sixth of my number?

I have **x + 1**.
Who has the square of my number?

I have **x^2 + 2x +1**.
Who has the # you would get if -x^2 - x - 4 is added to my #?

I have **x - 3**.
Who has twice my #?

I have **2x - 6**.
Who has 6 more than my #?

I have **2x**.
Who has the square of my number?

I have **4x^2**.
Who has my number decreased by 1?

I have $4x^2 - 1$.
Who has a factor of my number?

I have $2x + 1$.
Who has the value of this expression if $x = 4$?

I have 9.
Who has the product of my # and the square of x?

I have $9x^2$.
Who has a square root of my #?

I have $3x$.
Who has four times my number?

I have $12x$.
Who has the value of this expression if $x = \frac{1}{4}$?

I have **3**.
Who has the difference
of 3x and my number?

I have **3x −3**.
Who has one-third of
my number?

I have **x − 1**.
Who has the middle term
of the square of my #?

I have **−2x**.
Who has a number that is the
result if 9x is added to my #?

I have **7x**.
Who has a number 5
more than my number?

I have **7x + 5**.
Who has a # that is the result
if 5x is subtracted from my #?

I Have…Who Has? For Algebraic Expressions II

I Have $3(x+y)$.

Who Has three more than the quotient of x and y?

I Have $\dfrac{x}{y}+3$.

Who Has the product of x and y decreased by five?

I Have $xy-5$.

Who Has the sum of x squared and y squared?

I Have x^2+y^2.

Who Has y increased by three?

I Have $y+3$.

Who Has two decreased by x?

I Have $2-x$.

Who Has x minus three times y?

112

I Have $x - 3y$.

Who Has two less than x?

I Have $x - 2$.

Who Has one less than twice y?

I Have $2y - 1$.

Who Has three more than the product of x and y?

I Have $3 + xy$.

Who Has three less than the quotient of x and y?

I Have $\dfrac{x}{y} - 3$.

Who Has the difference between x and y?

I Have $x - y$.

Who Has four times the sum of three and x?

I Have $4(x+3)$.

Who Has four times x, increased by 3?

I Have $4x+3$.

Who Has the square of x decreased by one?

I Have x^2-1.

Who Has one subtracted from the cube of x?

I Have x^3-1.

Who Has one more than the square of x?

I Have x^2+1.

Who Has nine fewer than x?

I Have $x-9$.

Who Has two less than three times x?

I Have…Who Has? For Algebraic Expressions II

I Have $3x - 2$.

Who Has two more than x?

I Have $x + 2$.

Who Has y decreased by three?

I Have $y - 3$.

Who Has two times x plus three?

I Have $2x + 3$.

Who Has x divided by y?

I Have $\dfrac{x}{y}$.

Who Has the quotient of x and three?

I Have $\dfrac{x}{3}$.

Who Has three times x minus five?

I Have $3x - 5$.

Who Has three divided by the sum of x and 2?

I Have $\dfrac{3}{x+2}$.

Who Has five times the sum of x and 2?

I Have $5(x + 2)$.

Who Has nine more than x?

I Have $x + 9$.

Who Has five times the product of x and y?

I Have $5xy$.

Who Has the difference of xy and five?

I Have $xy - 5$.

Who Has three times the sum of x and y?

I Have…Who Has? For Geometric Terms

Cut out the strips and distribute them to the students.

I have <u>supplementary angles</u>. Who has a quadrilateral with both pairs of opposite sides parallel?	I have an <u>angle bisector</u>. Who has coplanar lines that do not intersect?
I have a <u>parallelogram</u>. Who has a parallelogram with four congruent sides but does not have four right angles?	I have <u>parallel lines.</u> Who has an angle whose measure is between 90^0 and 180^0?
I have a <u>rhombus</u>. Who has a parallelogram with four right angles but does not have four congruent sides?	I have an <u>obtuse angle.</u> Who has a line, segment or ray that is perpendicular to a segment at its midpoint?
I have a <u>rectangle</u>. Who has a parallelogram with four congruent sides and four right angles?	I have a <u>perpendicular bisector of a segment.</u> Who has what we call points that lie on the same line?
I have a <u>square.</u> Who has a quadrilateral with two pairs of adjacent sides congruent and no opposite sides congruent?	I have <u>collinear points.</u> Who has the part of a line consisting of one endpoint and all the points of the line on one side of the endpoint?
I have a <u>kite.</u> Who has a quadrilateral with exactly one pair of parallel sides?	I have a <u>ray.</u> Who has two lines that intersect to form right angles?
I have a <u>trapezoid.</u> Who has a trapezoid whose non-parallel opposite sides are congruent?	I have <u>perpendicular lines.</u> Who has a point that divides a segment into two congruent segments?

I Have…Who Has? For Geometric Terms

I have an <u>isosceles trapezoid.</u> Who has the two congruent sides of an isosceles triangle?	**I have the <u>midpoint of a segment.</u>** Who has the figure formed by two rays with the same endpoint?
I have the <u>legs</u>. Who has the angle formed by the two congruent sides of an isosceles triangle?	**I have an <u>angle.</u>** Who has two angles that have the same measure?
I have the <u>vertex angle.</u> Who has the side opposite the right angle of a right triangle?	**I have <u>congruent angles</u>.** Who has an angle measuring between 0^0 and 90^0?
I have the <u>hypotenuse</u>. Who has the angles of an isosceles triangle that are not the vertex angles?	**I have an <u>acute angle</u>.** Who has an angle measuring 180^0?
I have the <u>base angles</u>. Who has what we call the points, lines and figures that are in the same plane?	**I have a <u>straight angle</u>.** Who has an angle measuring 90^0?
I have <u>coplanar</u>. Who has the part of a line consisting of two endpoints and all points between them?	**I have a <u>right angle</u>.** Who has two coplanar angles with a common side, a common vertex and no common interior points?
I have a <u>line segment</u>. Who has what we call two segments with the same length?	**I have <u>adjacent angles</u>.** Who has two angles whose measures have a sum of 90^0?
I have <u>congruent segments</u>. Who has a ray that divides an angle into two congruent angles?	**I have <u>complementary angles</u>.** Who has two angles whose measures have a sum of 180^0?

Logarithm Formulas Sort It Out Game

Formulas:

1. $\log_b A + \log_b B = \log_b AB$
2. $\log_b A - \log_b B = \log_b(A/B)$
3. $\log_b A^k = k\log_b A$

After having taught the logarithm formulas and having shown examples of them, divide the class into groups of 2-3. Give each group an envelope containing the sample cards shown below written on index cards cut in half. Students are given 3-5 minutes to make as many correct mathematical equations out of the cards in the envelope as they can in the time allowed. Some cards might be unused. At the end of the allowed time, find the two groups that have the most equations and check to make sure that they are all mathematically correct. Each member of these groups will earn bonus points, candy, or "late homework" passes.

Then have each group read out one equation they created, as the teacher writes the equations on the board, grouping similar types of equations together. Continue putting the equations on the board until no group has a different equation to offer that is not already posted.

Sample Cards:

$\log_3 24$	$2\log_3 2$	$\log_3 6$	$5\log_2 2$	$\log_2 2$
$\log_2 16$	$\log_3 10$	$\log_3 2$	$\log_3 20$	$\log_4 15$

$\log_4 3$	$\log_4 5$	$3\log_2 2$	$\log_2 8$	$\log_2 4$

+	+	−	—	=

=	+	=	+	=

—	=

Partner Relay Races

Directions:

Students should move their desks side-by-side with a partner and group four (or five) partner groups into a row to form a team. Make one copy of the race for each team. Distribute the copy, face down, to the first partner group in each team. If there are not enough partner groups to evenly distribute over the teams, then the paper can be passed back up a row to finish the commands. On the Go! command the first group should complete the directions for Partner Group 1, write down their answer, and then pass the paper over their head to the Partner Group 2 in their team. This group follows the directions for Partner Group 2 and passes the paper on to the next group. This continues until the last group in the team gets the paper. When the last group in the team has completely written down their answer, they should raise their hands. Check the answer in the order in which the hands were raised for the different teams in the room. The first group to have the correct answer earns a bonus point (or prize) for each member of their team. If a team gets an incorrect answer, tell the team to gather around the back set of desks to try to correct their answer until a winner is declared.

Polynomial Race

Start with: $3x^2 - 2x - 3$

Partner Group 1:

Add $-6x^2 - 4x + 3$ to the starting polynomial.   Answer: _____

Partner Group 2:

Add $-6x - 4$ to the last answer.   Answer:_____

Partner Group 3:

Add $4x^2 - 2x + 3$ to the last answer.   Answer: _____

Partner Group 4:

Add $2x^2 + 4x - 6$ to the last answer.   Answer: _____

Partner Group 5:

Add $-x^2 + 3x + 4$ to the last answer.   Answer: _____

Radical Race 1

<u>Start with:</u> $2\sqrt{7}$

Partner Group 1:

Add $6\sqrt{28}$ to the starting radical.   Answer: _____

Partner Group 2:

Subtract $\sqrt{63}$ from the last answer.   Answer: _____

Partner Group 3:

Subtract $\sqrt{28}$ from the last answer.   Answer: _____

Partner Group 4:

Add $3\sqrt{63}$ to the last answer.   Answer: _____

Partner Group 5:

Subtract $2\sqrt{28}$ from the last answer.   Answer: _____

Radical Race 2

<u>Start with:</u> $\sqrt{20} - \sqrt{24}$

Partner Group 1:

Add $2\sqrt{54}$ to the starting radical.   Answer: _____

Partner Group 2:

Subtract $2\sqrt{54}$ from the last answer.   Answer: _____

Partner Group 3:

Add $6\sqrt{54}$ to the last answer.   Answer: _____

Partner Group 4:

Subtract $3\sqrt{45}$ from the last answer.   Answer: _____

Partner Group 5:

Add $4\sqrt{20}$ to the last answer.   Answer: _____

Derivative Race 1

Start with: $f(x) = -2x^5 - 2x^4 - x^{-2} + 4$

Partner Group 1:
Find f′(x) of the start polynomial.　　　Answer: _____

Partner Group 2:
Find f″(x) of the start polynomial.　　　Answer: _____

Partner Group 3:
Find f‴(x) of the start polynomial.　　　Answer: _____
Partner Group 4:
Find f″″(x) of the start polynomial.　　　Answer: _____

Derivative Race 2

Start with: $y = \cos 2x$
Partner Group 1:
Find f′(x) of the start polynomial.　　　Answer: _____
Partner Group 2:
Find f″(x) of the start polynomial.　　　Answer: _____
Partner Group 3:
Find f‴(x) of the start polynomial.　　　Answer: _____
Partner Group 4:
Find f″″(x) of the start polynomial.　　　Answer: _____

PARTNER RELAY RACES ANSWER KEY

POLYNOMIAL RACE

Partner Group 1: $-3x^2 - 6x$
Partner Group 2: $-3x^2 - 12x - 4$
Partner Group 3: $x^2 - 14x - 1$
Partner Group 4: $3x^2 - 10x - 7$
Partner Group 5: $2x^2 - 7x - 3$

RADICAL RACE 1

Partner Group 1: $14\sqrt{7}$
Partner Group 2: $11\sqrt{7}$
Partner Group 3: $9\sqrt{7}$
Partner Group 4: $18\sqrt{7}$
Partner Group 5: $14\sqrt{7}$

RADICAL RACE 2

Partner Group 1: $2\sqrt{5} + 4\sqrt{6}$
Partner Group 2: $2\sqrt{5} - 2\sqrt{6}$
Partner Group 3: $2\sqrt{5} + 16\sqrt{6}$
Partner Group 4: $-7\sqrt{5} + 16\sqrt{6}$
Partner Group 5: $\sqrt{5} + 16\sqrt{6}$

DERIVATIVE RACE 1

Partner Group 1: $-10x^4 - 8x^3 + 2x^{-3}$
Partner Group 2: $-40x^3 - 24x^2 - 6x^{-4}$
Partner Group 3: $-120x^2 - 48x + 24x^{-5}$
Partner Group 4: $-240x - 48 - 120x^{-6}$

DERIVATIVE RACE 2

Partner Group 1: $-2\sin 2x$
Partner Group 2: $-4\cos 2x$
Partner Group 3: $8\sin 2x$

Partner Group 4: $16\cos 2x$

The Fishing Game for Graphing Linear Equations

Directions for making the game:

❑ Print approximately 20 copies of the fish template.

❑ Create about 40 problems and answers that match to your unit of study. More or fewer problems might be necessary depending on the size of your class and the number of teams.

❑ Cut out the problems and answers and tape or glue each one of them to the back side of a fish. Use one shape of fish on which to paste the questions and one shape on which to paste the answers. Laminate before cutting out, if possible.

❑ Either lay the fish (problem and answer sides up) on a table at the front of the room or attach magnetic tape to the front side of the fish and post them on the white board in the classroom. Separately put all the questions together on the left and all the answers together on the right.

Directions for playing the game:

❑ Form teams of 4-5 students. Each team will choose two runners from their group.

❑ Each team will send "Runner #1" to go select a fish problem.

❑ The team works the problem together and sends "Runner #2" to go find the correct answer that matches to the problem. The runner has to verify their selection with the teacher before returning to their team with the matching fish.

❑ **Only if the runner has chosen the correct fish and shown it to the teacher does that team get to claim the match. If an incorrect match is made, the team has to return the problem fish and answer fish and choose a different problem.**

❑ **At any time during the game a team may decide that a problem is too difficult and choose to send their "Runner #1" to return it and choose another problem.**

❑ The team that catches the most fish at the end of the game is the winner. **Bonus points or candy or "late" homework passes can be given to the members of the winning team.**

❑ **Students could be asked to turn in a record of their team work on paper for a participation grade if the teacher thinks this is necessary to ensure that each team is working effectively.**

Answer Key for The Fishing Game on Recognizing the Graphs of Linear Functions:

The problems each have an assigned letter of the alphabet and each graph has an assigned number. The matches are listed below for the teacher to use for quick checking as the game is being played.

A 15	D 12	G 20	J 17	M 4	P 1	S 7
B 14	E 11	H 19	K 16	N 3	Q 9	T 6
C 13	F 10	I 18	L 5	O 2	R 8	

The Fishing Game on Recognizing the Graphs of Linear Functions

Problems to Graph:
$5x - 3y = 15$ **A**
$y = -2.5$ **B**
$2x - 5y = 10$ **C**
$x + y = 2$ **D**

15

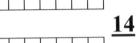

14

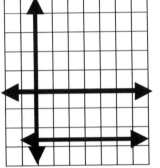

13

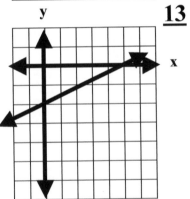

12

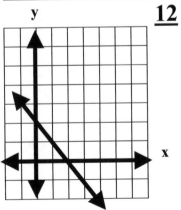

126

The Fishing Game on Recognizing the Graphs of Linear Functions

Problems to Graph:
$4x + 3y = 12$
E
$y - x = 5$
F
$x - 2y = -6$
G
$x = 3$
H

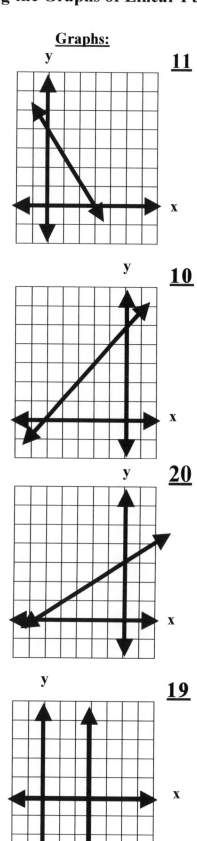

Graphs:

11

10

20

19

The Fishing Game on Recognizing the Graphs of Linear Functions

Graphs:

Problems to Graph:
$2x - 3y = -9$
I
$4x + 3y = 15$
J
$x - 3y = -3$
K
$x - y = 0$
L

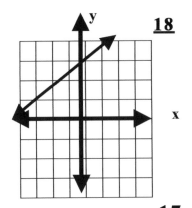

18

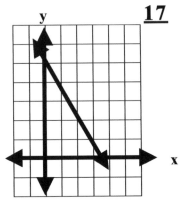

17

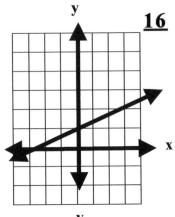

16

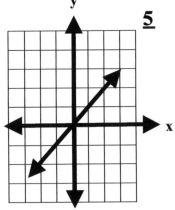

5

The Fishing Game on Recognizing the Graphs of Linear Functions

Problems to Graph:
$2x - y = 5$ <u>M</u>
$x + 2y = -2$ <u>N</u>
$y = 4$ <u>O</u>
$x + y = 0$ <u>P</u>

Graphs:

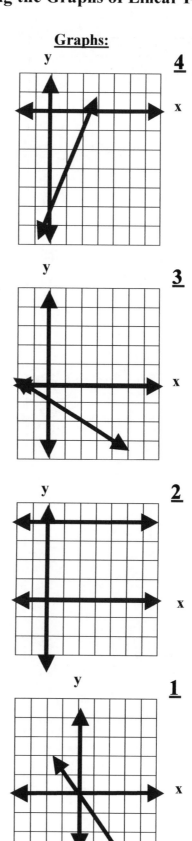

The Fishing Game on Recognizing the Graphs of Linear Functions

Problems to Graph:	
$2x + y = 0$	**Q**
$x + y = 3$	**R**
$x - y = -2$	**S**
$2x + 3y = -6$	**T**

Graphs

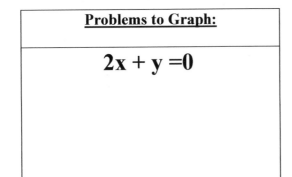

9
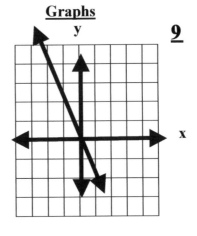

8
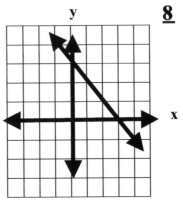

7

6
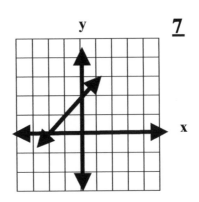

130

The Fishing Game on Recognizing the Graphs of Conic Sections

Graphs:

Problems:

A.

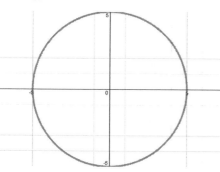

10.

$$x^2 + y^2 = 25$$

B.

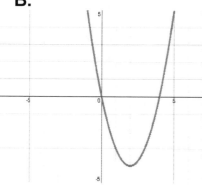

9.

$$y = (x - 2)^2 - 4$$

C.

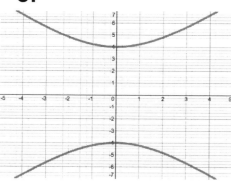

8.

$$\frac{y^2}{16} - \frac{x^2}{9} = 1$$

D.

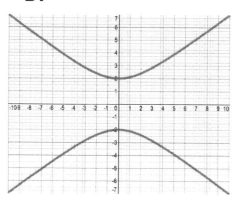

6.

$$\frac{y^2}{4} - \frac{x^2}{9} = 1$$

The Fishing Game on Recognizing the Graphs of Conic Sections

Graphs:

Problems:

E.

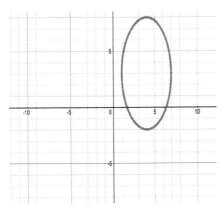

7.

$$\frac{(x-4)^2}{9} + \frac{(y-3)^2}{25} = 1$$

4.

F.

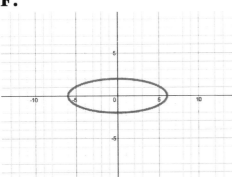

$$\frac{x^2}{36} + \frac{y^2}{4} = 1$$

G.

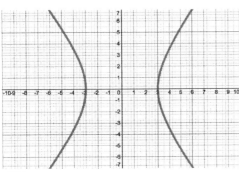

5.

$$\frac{x^2}{9} - \frac{y^2}{16} = 1$$

H.

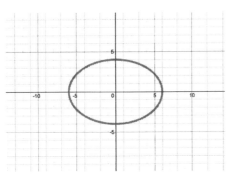

2.

$$\frac{x^2}{36} + \frac{y^2}{16} = 1$$

132

The Fishing Game on Recognizing the Graphs of Conic Sections

Graphs:

Problems

I.

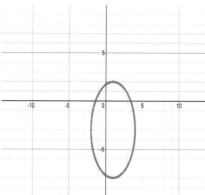

3.

$$\frac{(x-1)^2}{25} + \frac{(y+3)^2}{9} = 1$$

J.

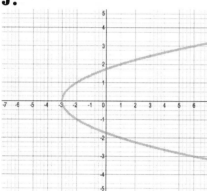

12.

$$x = y^2 - 3$$

K.

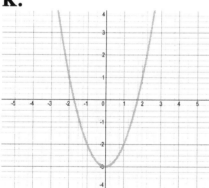

11.

$$y = x^2 - 3$$

<u>**Answer Key for The Fishing Game on Recognizing the Graphs of Conic Sections:**</u>

The problems each have an assigned letter of the alphabet and each graph has an assigned number. The matches are listed below for the teacher to use for quick checking as the game is being played.

A 10	D 6	G 5	J 12
B 9	E 7	H 2	K 11
C 8	F 4	I 3	

The Fishing Game on Recognizing the Graphs of Quadratic Functions

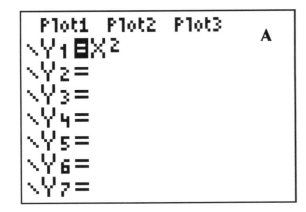

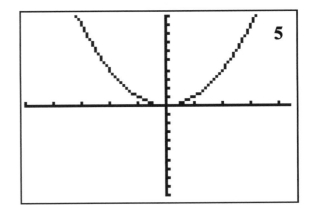

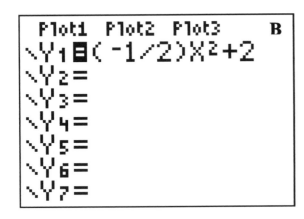

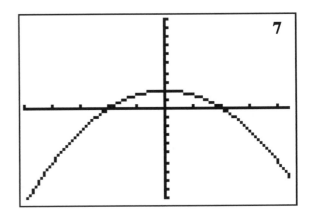

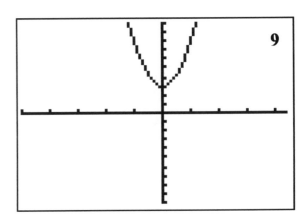

The Fishing Game on Recognizing the Graphs of Quadratic Functions

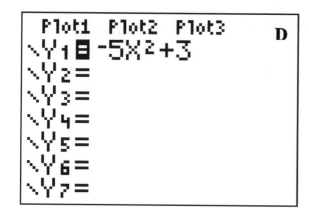

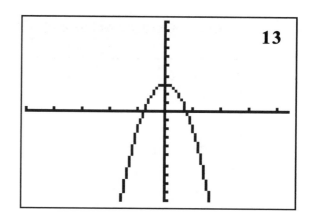

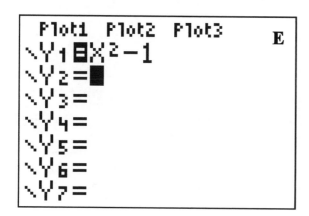

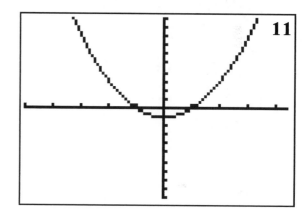

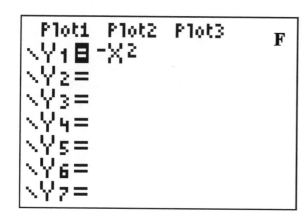

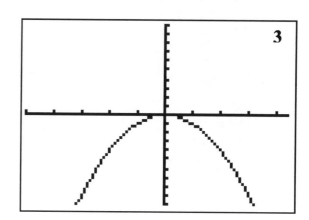

The Fishing Game on Recognizing the Graphs of Quadratic Functions

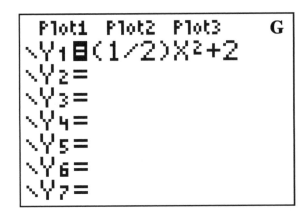

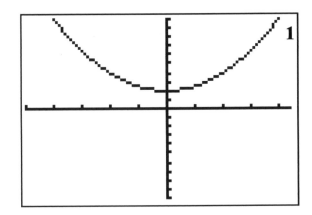

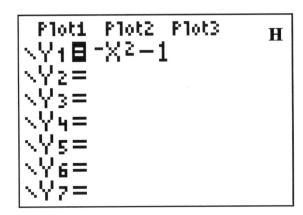

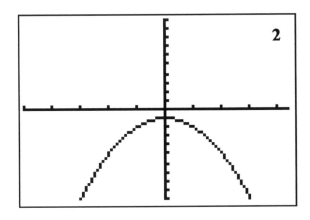

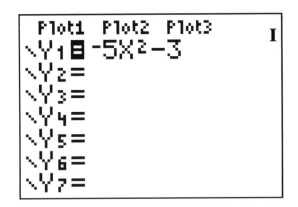

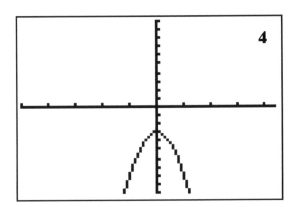

The Fishing Game on Recognizing the Graphs of Quadratic Functions

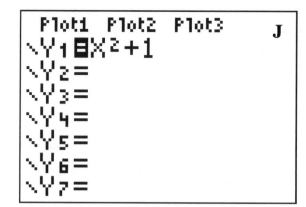

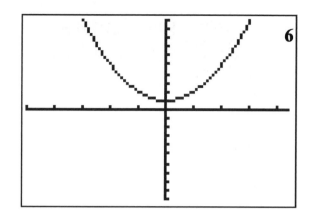

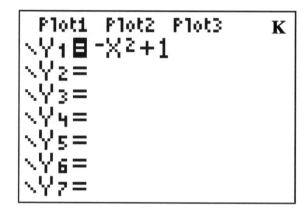

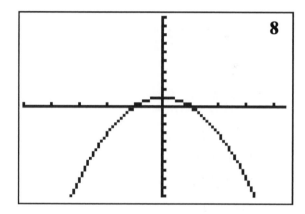

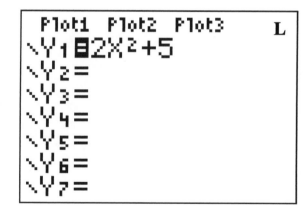

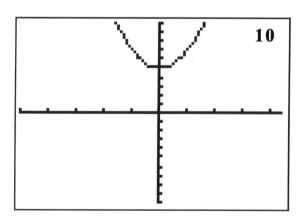

The Fishing Game on Recognizing the Graphs of Quadratic Functions

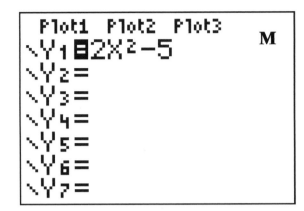

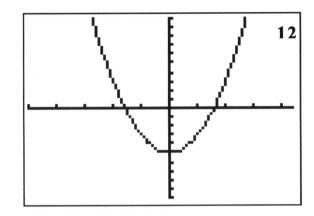

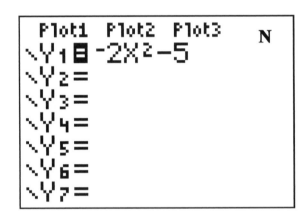

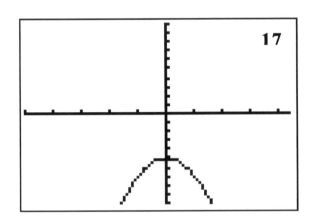

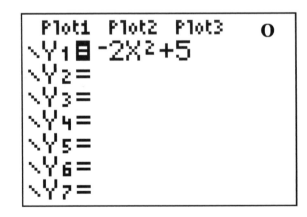

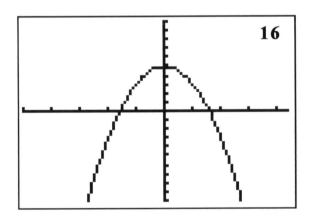

The Fishing Game on Recognizing the Graphs of Quadratic Functions

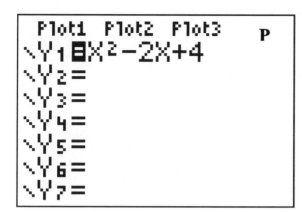

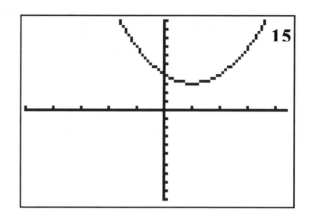

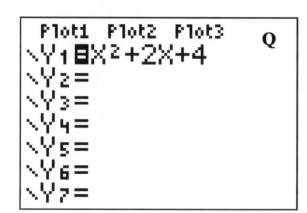

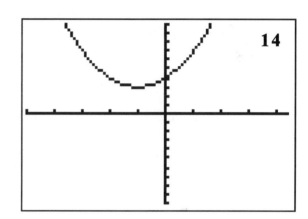

Answer Key for The Fishing Game on Recognizing the Graphs of Quadratic Functions

The problems each have an assigned letter of the alphabet and each graph has an assigned number. The matches are listed below for the teacher to use for quick checking as the game is being played.

A 5	D 13	G 1	J 6	M 12	P 15
B 7	E 11	H 2	K 8	N 17	Q 14
C 9	F 3	I 4	L 10	O 16	

Concentration Math

Concentration Math is played similar to the old Television game show called Concentration. It is a matching game for the purpose of practicing comparing and identifying equivalent amounts. Students are grouped to play as individuals or as a pair. A group of 2 to 8 may plan with one set of cards taking turns in a clockwise manner. Some teachers have even divided the class into 2 teams to play. It is important to periodically stop and have pairs softly share what they know and why.

A set of cars with matching equivalences will be needed. Cards must be randomly placed in a matrix or array with letters facing upward and equivalences facing downward. When it is their turn, a player or pair may turn over 2 cards (if larger group, the 2 cards may be called out and a designated person will turn the cards). If the written values on the cards are equivalent, the pair (player) collects the cards and they get another turn. If the card values are not equivalent, the pair turn the cards back over, and it is the next team's turn. Play until all cards have been matched. The pair (player) who collects the most cards is the winner. To win, players have to pay attention to each turn of cards and remember the location of cards with the same value.

Concentration Math: Operations with Exponents

$\dfrac{5^6}{5^4}$	5^2	$(3^2)^3$
$3^2 \cdot 3^3$	3^5	3^6
$a^3 \cdot a$	a^4	$\left(\dfrac{2}{3}\right)^3$

$\left(\dfrac{a^2}{b}\right)^2$	$\dfrac{a^4}{b^2}$	$\dfrac{8}{27}$
$2^{\frac{1}{2}} \cdot 2^{\frac{1}{2}}$	2	$\dfrac{b^5}{b^4}$
$a^2 + a^2$	$2a^2$	b

$$\frac{2^3}{4^2}$$

$$\frac{8}{16}$$

-32

$$\frac{a^6}{b^3}$$

$$\left(\frac{a^2}{b}\right)^3$$

$$\frac{(-4)^3}{2}$$

$$\left(-\frac{1}{2}\right)^3$$

$$-\frac{1}{8}$$

Concentration Math: Fractions, Decimals, Percents

7 hundredths	0.07	$\dfrac{2.5}{5}$
11	$\dfrac{121}{11}$	50%
$\dfrac{6}{1.2}$	5	0.45

$\dfrac{3}{6}$	0.5	$\dfrac{45}{100}$
$0.33\overline{3}$	$\dfrac{1}{3}$	$\dfrac{5}{6}$
$\dfrac{3}{3}$	100%	$\dfrac{15}{18}$

$\dfrac{3}{4}$	75%	$\dfrac{1}{4}$
$\dfrac{4}{5}$	$\dfrac{16}{20}$	25%
	$\dfrac{2}{5}$	0.40

$5\sqrt{7} + 2\sqrt{7}$	$7\sqrt{7}$	$\sqrt{8} + \sqrt{2}$
$\sqrt{3}\,(2 + \sqrt{3})$	$2\sqrt{3} + 3$	$3\sqrt{2}$
$\sqrt{x^2 + 2x + 1}$	$X + 1$	$\sqrt{2}(\sqrt{2} + 1)$

$7\sqrt{2} - \sqrt{2}$	$6\sqrt{2}$	$2 + \sqrt{2}$
$(3\sqrt{2})(5\sqrt{2})$	30	$\sqrt[3]{8 \cdot 27}$
$\sqrt[4]{\dfrac{5^4}{2^5}}$	$\dfrac{5}{2\sqrt[4]{2}}$	6

$x\sqrt{45} - x\sqrt{5}$	$2x\sqrt{5}$	$\dfrac{12}{\sqrt{3}} + 2\sqrt{3}$
$\sqrt[4]{\dfrac{(20)^2}{81}}$	$\dfrac{2\,(\sqrt[4]{25})}{3}$	$6\sqrt{3}$
	$\dfrac{-2\,(8)}{\sqrt{2}}$	$-8\sqrt{2}$

Twenty Questions on Equations of Circles

This activity requires deductive reasoning on the part of the student as he or she recognizes equations of circles. The teacher presents the students with a set of the graphs of the following equations and informs students that he/she has written an equation for one of them on a sticky note. This is an especially good activity for pairs. Give time before starting for the pairs to make notes about what they know about each of the following equations. Then choose a pair to ask yes or no questions of the teacher until one pair names the correct equation. Give time between each question asked for pairs to discuss what equations that they can eliminate after getting the yes or no answer to their question. The pair receives a bonus point or prize of some sort when they are able to pick the correct equation on the teacher's sticky note.

$(x-3)^3 + (y-4)^2 + 6 = 31$ $(x-2)^2 + (y-1)^2 - 6 = 30$

$(x-3)^2 + (y+4)^2 = 36$ $(x-3)^2 + (y-1)^2 = 4$

$3x^2 + 3y^2 = 27$ $x^2 + y^2 = 36$

$x^2 + y^2 + 8x - 2y - 8 = 0$ $x^2 + y^2 + 4 = 8$

$2x^2 + 2y^2 = 50$ $(x-2)^2 + (y-1)^2 = 9$

Guess My Rule

Curriculum Objective: Identify properties and relationships of data in tables, graphs, and equations.

This is a guessing game played by the teacher against the class. The teacher displays a large T chart on the board or screen. Then the teacher tells the students that he or she is thinking of a rule of a line that takes any number that is chosen for x, operates on the number using the rule, and then produces a answer called y. The teacher then chooses one student to suggest a number for x. Then they tell the class what number is generated for y after the chosen rule operates on their x. Record the corresponding x and y values on the T chart. Play continues as the teacher asks random students to suggest an x, with the teacher then supplying the value of y that corresponds to their x under the rule of which they were thinking.

Students are told to raise their hand when they want to guess the rule but not to say out loud what they think the rule is. Instead, the teacher will give them an x and they have to say what y would be produced under the rule of which they are thinking. The teacher is to look for the first three hands in the order that they are raised, noting one, two, and three order. A prize or bonus point is given to the first student who can name the correctly stated rule. When the rule is guessed correctly, with the entire class, the teacher then will graph the ordered pairs that have resulted from the game and connect the points to form the line named by the corresponding equation. Strategies will be discussed for recognizing the rule in an easier manner for the next game.

Guess My Graph

Curriculum Objectives: Find the slope of a line given the graph of the line, an equation of the line, or two points on the line; Write the equation of and graph linear relationships given two points on the line.

The teacher needs to prepare ahead of time the graph on a line on a coordinate plane but he or she does not show it to the class until the game begins. In the beginning, the line needs to have two clearly marked points on the line with one of them being the y-intercept. Of course this can be changed to make the game more difficult as students get more accustomed to the game.

Before starting the game the teacher needs to explain to the students that they will be shown the graph of a line. The students are to guess the equation of the line, putting their answer in slope-intercept form. The teacher instructs the students to write down their guess, and then as soon as their guess is written down, to raise their hand to indicate they want to guess an answer. The teacher is to look for the first three hands in the order that they are raised, noting one, two, and three order. The teacher displays the graph to begin the game, and then cuts off the display of the graph before students are chosen to answer, to encourage them to have had a written answer. A prize or bonus point is given to the first student who can name the equation of the graphed line. The teacher should ask the student naming the correct answer to explain their strategy as to how they figured out the answer so quickly. Then the play continues with a new graph.

Wheel of Mathematics Game Directions

Based on the game show, "Wheel of Fortune", the Wheels game format forces students to repeatedly reflect on steps in a process. Students use numerous problem solving skills and higher thinking skills while playing the game. The game may be played with the class divided into two groups or pairs of students playing against each other. The teacher works out a problem and puts the pattern on the board.

Example:

$$\boxed{} X^2 \pm \boxed{} \; \boxed{} x \pm \boxed{} = \boxed{} (\boxed{} x \pm \boxed{})(\boxed{} x \pm \boxed{})$$

Divide the class into two teams. A pair or group on the first team picks a number from 0-9. Example: Are there any 5s? If so, the teacher will write all the 5s in the appropriate boxes and give the team a point for each.

5 $x^2 \pm \square \; \square \; x \pm \square = \square$ (**5** $x \pm \square$) ($\square x \pm \square$) The team gets 2 points.

Then it is the other team's turn. The teacher may choose to write the numbers given by each team in different colors. After a couple of numbers have been added to the game board, stop and let pairs talk quietly about what they know and their next number pick. Occasionally ask students what they know at that point and how they know. This provides struggling students with insights into the relationships in the equation and the type of thinking they may try. Teams take turns picking numbers until all the boxes are filled in. At first, do not let a team tell the answer even if they know; this provides more practice for struggling learners. After a few rounds, a team may guess the example and receive an extra 5 points. However, incorrect guessing costs a team 3 points. Note that students giving the final answer must name the correct signs as well or the other team gets a chance to name the answer. The team with the most points wins.

Wheel of Factors

Teacher and Students draw the following playing board:

Game Format

$$\square \, X^2 \pm \square \, \square x \pm \square = \square \, (\square x \pm \square \,)(\square \, x \pm \square \,)$$

Game One

$$3\, x^2 - 02x - 8 = 1\,(3x + 4)\,(1x - 2)$$

Game Two:

$$5\, x^2 + 13x - 6 = 1\,(5x - 2)\,(1x + 3)$$

Game Three:

$$4\, x^2 \pm 00\, x - 9 = 1\,(2x - 3)\,(2x + 3)$$

Game Four:

$$4\, x^2 + 11x + 6 = 1\,(4x + 3)\,(1x + 2)$$

Game Format:

$$\square \, a^2 \pm \square \, \square \, ab \pm \square \, b^2 = \square \, (\square \, a \pm \square \, b)(\square \, a \pm \square \, b)$$

Game Five:

$$9\, a^2 + 00\, ab + 4\, b^2 = 1(3a + 2\, b)\,(3a - 2b)$$

Game Six:

$$3\, a^2 - 10ab + 8b^2 = 1(3a - 4b)\,(1a - 2b)$$

154

Wheel of Polynomial Division

Game Format Sample:

$$\frac{\square\, a^{\square} - \square\, a^{\square} + \square\, a^{\square}}{a^{\square}} = \square\, a^{\square} - \square\, a^{\square} + \frac{\square\, a^{\square}}{\square\, a^{\square}}$$

Game One:

$$\frac{1a^5 - 5a^2 + 3a^1}{a^2} = 1a^3 - 5a^0 + \frac{3}{a^1}$$

Game Two:

$$\frac{-15x^3 + 30x^2 + 5x^1}{5x^1} = -3x^2 + 6x^1 + 1x^0$$

Game Three:

$$\frac{6n^5 - 12n^3 + 3n^1}{3n^1} = 2n^4 - 4n^2 + 1n^0$$

Game Four:

$$\frac{9c^2 - 12cd + 6cd^2}{3cd} = \frac{3c - 4}{d} + 2d$$

Made in the USA
San Bernardino, CA
11 August 2016